The Life and
Death of Whales

The Life and
Death of
Whales

Robert Burton

 ANDRE DEUTSCH

First published March 1973 by
André Deutsch Limited
105 Great Russell Street London WC1

Second edition, revised and
enlarged, 1980

Printed in Great Britain by
Ebenezer Baylis & Son Ltd
The Trinity Press, Worcester, and London

ISBN 0 233 97130 0

Contents

List of Illustrations

ACKNOWLEDGEMENTS

Many writers have set down their experiences
of whales or whaling, or have gathered
together obscure or scattered observations.
This book draws together a sample of the
immense stock of information that exists.
Like similar books it cannot cover the whole
and it relies heavily on published works by
authors who have already shed light on the
habits of whales and their pursuit by man.
I am indebted to these authors, and also to
Nigel Bonner who gave me the benefit of his
knowledge.

PART I | The Life of Whales

God seems to have made the whale as a proof of his power. It is in every respect the finest animal in nature. Whatever care we take to imagine a large animal beforehand, yet the first sight of this huge creature never fails to strike us with astonishment and awe. Having been used to smaller animals, we have no conception of its enormous magnitude: for a moving column of flesh 120 feet long and 75 feet in circumference is an object so utterly different from those we are constantly presented with, that, to be comprehended, it must actually be seen: but the skeleton of the whale is by far a finer subject of curiosity than the whale itself; the whale, at first view, presents the spectator with an enormous mass of flesh, and scarcely seems animated, until pursued by the swordfish, or struck by the harpooner. When, however, the mass of flesh is removed, and the skeleton stands confessed and exposed, as it now does in Gloucester Green, it is then that we acknowledge that 'those who go down to the sea in ships see the wonders of the deep', and that there is no mechanical structure to be compared with the skeleton of the whale.

When the illustrious Galen examined a similar skeleton, he suddenly became converted from the errors of Atheism. Who can contemplate this mighty skeleton, without adoring the Mind that formed it? Where can we better cultivate a sentiment of devotion than in the presence of work so expressive of the various attributes of the varied God?

From a nineteenth-century handbill advertising the exhibition of a whale skeleton

1 | Whales Defined and Described

WHALES have become popular animals in the last ten or so years. Public interest was first aroused when their plight at the hands of the whalers became widely known through the agitation of conservationists. Public debate and demonstration drew attention to the fact, little appreciated, that for years whales had been turned into pet food, so the family cat and dog had been fed on the flesh of animals of equal intelligence and sensibility. These warm-blooded, graceful animals, awe-inspiring in their sheer bulk, have provided more than pet food. Products from their body tissues used to pervade our lives. They found their way into soaps and cosmetics, lubricating oils, paints and varnishes, inks and detergents, leather and food. Public pressure and the dwindling numbers of whales left to supply an expanding market has led to a gradual but as yet incomplete replacement of whale products with materials from other sources.

The exploitation of whales as a resource might not have been too worrying but for two reasons. Most of us accept the exploitation of cattle, sheep and pigs, but farm animals are killed humanely and are managed rationally. Whaling fails on these two counts. Chasing and harpooning whales is not an abattoir operation and the whaling industry has not been under particularly rational management. Its history is a succession of ruthless commercial plunderings. Species after species, population after population, have been hunted out, and even eleventh-hour attempts at international control of the industry have largely failed to stem the destruction of animals which can be seen either as one of the wonders of the natural world or a major renewable source of raw material.

The growth of public concern over whales has been assisted by their becoming more familiar. They appear as images on television screens in natural history programmes, and live as entertainers in dolphinaria. Wild whales even become seaside tourist attractions.

Public appreciation of whales has been matched by a surge of scientific investigation into their lives and habits. Traditionally zoologists have studied whales by dissection of their carcases and, while improved techniques are being brought into the study of anatomy and physiology, there are exciting new studies of living, wild whales. Whales live underwater in the vastness of the oceans, breaking the surface for hasty gulps of air, and their lives are very private. There used to be no good way of eavesdropping on whales, but the smaller species are now being watched in the confines of dolphinaria and large whales are followed in the open sea by light aircraft, small boats and even SCUBA divers. Many fascinating glimpses of whale life have been revealed but, at the moment, they are usually so brief that they are not easy to interpret and we are still a very long way from a complete understanding of whales. Only in recent years have we learnt the true shape of live whales. They were always depicted as having baggy throats, instead of being streamlined, because the throat sags after death.

The whales belong to the mammalian order of Cetacea, a group of animals which includes the large whales, such as the blue, fin and sperm whales, the smaller whales, such as the killer and pilot whales, and the various porpoises and dolphins. All live in water and all have roughly the same shape: a streamlined, fish-shaped body with flippers and flukes for propulsion. Many of them have been hunted, mainly for their blubber, which is rendered down to oil, and for their meat. Hunting of the larger whales developed into an important industry yet, because of their inaccessibility, less is known about their lives than those of their small relatives, the porpoises and dolphins. Porpoises and dolphins are going to be largely ignored in this book in favour of the larger whales which have been the mainstay of the whaling industry. The first part of the book attempts to set forth the lives of whales, while the second records the history and present state of their deaths at the hands of the whalers.

Whales are familiar animals; they are as much a part of our general knowledge as lions and tigers and elephants and hippopotamuses. Yet a true definition of whales has proved a problem to zoologists and laymen alike for centuries and it is still not properly resolved. When men started to name and classify animals they grouped them on the basis of external appearance and so made many mistakes about the true relationships. The whales were classed as fishes because they lived in the sea and had fins but no fur. Such a classification had a very practical use as it meant that whale flesh could be eaten during Lent. The development of a 'natural' system of classification came slowly. John Ray and Francis Willughby, the seventeenth-century founders of scientific natural history, divided the fishes into two sorts. The true fishes had gills, but the cetaceous fishes, which had a similar body plan, naked skin and marine life, possessed lungs instead of gills. The basis of the natural system as it stands today was worked out by the Swedish naturalist Linnaeus in the eighteenth century. Linnaeus classed whales as mammals, a term that was first coined by him in 1773 to cover the four-footed, furry animals, then known loosely as beasts, and their less obvious relatives such as bats and whales. The name only came into popular use about fifty years later.

If one agrees with the definition of a fish as an animal with a streamlined body, living in the water and swimming by means of fins, a whale is undoubtedly a fish. Herman Melville, the author of *Moby Dick*, pronounced that 'a whale is a spouting fish with a horizontal tail'. It is not a scientific definition, but it is only in recent years that people outside the small band of specialists have been expected to think about animals in scientific terms. As far as whalers were concerned, their quarry were 'fish' and they talked of 'fishing grounds' and 'fisheries' (when looking for books on whaling it is even advisable to search those shelves devoted to works on angling). This is fair enough for those employed in killing whales, where 'fish' is a technical term used by the profession, but it is a bad starting point for discussion of the biology of whales, where an understanding of the whale's place in the animal kingdom is essential.

Linnaeus classed the whales as mammals because they have features common to other mammals. They are warm-blooded, they have a double heart with two auricles and two ventricles, they breathe air with lungs, they bear their young alive and suckle them, and they even have traces of hair. To think of them as fishes, cold-blooded, breathing with gills and covered with scales, now seems ridiculous, as Aristotle realized in the fourth century BC. His wisdom was ignored for centuries.

Our understanding of the relationships of animals and their proper position in the evolutionary scale has come from the study of anatomy, or body structure, in which we can see that closely related animals have similar bodies, particularly in the form of the skeleton. Study of the skeleton is particularly important because the skeletons of extinct animals have survived as fossils and it is often possible to find fossils of animals that are common ancestors to animals alive today.

The search for an ancestor of the whales and a clue to their relationship to other mammals has proved difficult. They are so well adapted for life in the sea, with the all-important skeleton being modified for swimming rather than walking, that it is barely possible even to point to a distant land-living relative. All the fossils of whales that have been unearthed to date are of animals that are distinctly whales and show few traces of features that would link them with a land-living ancestor. The oldest fossil whales come from a group which flourished in the Eocene period about sixty million years ago. They were strange eel-like animals which grew up to twenty metres long. From their skulls and teeth it would appear that the ancestors of the whales were the creodonts, a primitive, long-extinct group of mammals which also gave rise to the cloven-hoofed mammals, such as cattle, sheep and deer, and the carnivores.

When a whale is examined in detail the changes that have taken place to transform it from a land animal to a marine animal become clear. Its shape, its skeleton, its means of propulsion, the workings of the respiratory system and the sense organs have undergone profound changes. At first sight they may appear to be quite unrelated to the equivalent parts of a land mammal but they are based on the same plan. There has been a programme of modification rather than of replacement in the evolution of the whales, except in the organs of propulsion where the limbs of a land mammal have been replaced by the fluked tail. These changes are described in a

later chapter, but the basic form of a whale must be understood and the different kinds of whales described before making
any detailed examination of their lives and habits.

The striking feature of whales, when compared with any
other group of mammals, is their extreme size. Life in the sea,
with the body supported on all sides by a cushion of water,
releases them from the restraints that gravity imposes on land
animals. No set of limbs of a conventional form could support
the body of a whale-sized land animal. The actual size of a
large whale is not easy to comprehend. A few blue whales, the
largest species, have been found to measure over 30 metres
long and weigh over 150 tonnes. These animals can be equated
with a herd of elephants or 1,500 men, but such comparisons do
not readily convey an impression of the bulk of such a creature.
A better way of appreciating their size is to walk round a life
size model of a whale, like the blue whales displayed at the
Natural History Museum in South Kensington and the
American Museum of Natural History. It is no wonder that
the writer of the handbill quoted at the head of this chapter
should expound so eloquently on the size of his exhibit and
consider that it was a practical lesson in divinity.

An even more evocative account of the size of these animals
comes from the dissection of a stranded whale described by
Francis Buckland:

> He [the dissector] carefully descended into the gigantic
> mass of anatomical horrors, and took out what parts he
> wanted. This service was not, however, done without danger,
> for when dissecting the enormous heart his foot slipped, and
> he fell into one of the cavities of the heart, his feet passing
> down into the great artery, the aorta. Assistance was luckily
> at hand, or he might have met with a fatal accident. To
> show the narrow escape he had, he subsequently cut rings
> out of this aorta, and found that he could pass them, without
> stretching, over his head and shoulders right down to his
> feet.

A large part of the whale's bulk is composed of a thick layer of
blubber which keeps the body warm, acts as a food reserve and
gives the whale its streamlined appearance. The head is large
and almost free of blubber which becomes very thick just

behind the head so that it disguises the short neck and smooths out the lines of the body. The shape of the head is distinctly odd when compared with that of the head of a horse or a dog. Nostrils at the tip of the muzzle have been replaced by 'blowholes' on top of the head; the eyes are set well down the sides of the head; and the mouth has a long, grinning gape. At first sight it seems as if the air passages must connect with the blowhole through the middle of the brain, but the head has not been quite so drastically reorganized. There has merely been a reshaping of the skull, some parts being enlarged and others being reduced. The effect has been to shorten the muzzle (the nasal bone) so that the nostrils are now close against the braincase (Figure 1). At the same time the bone forming the upper lip (the premaxilla) is greatly enlarged to form a secondary muzzle or 'beak' in which the rows of teeth or whalebone plates are embedded.

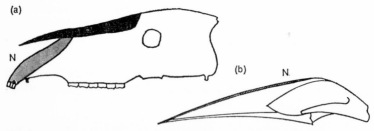

Figure 1 Skulls of (a) a horse and (b) a whalebone whale, to show the changes undergone by whales. ■ – nasal bone, ▨ – premaxilla, N – nostril or blowhole.

The streamlining of a whale is broken by as few obstructions as on a jet aeroplane. There is a pair of flippers behind the head, a pair of flukes on the tail and, in many species, there is a fin in the middle of the back. The flippers are the last visible remains of the two pairs of limbs owned by the whale's unknown ancestor. From the arm or leg of a land animal the whale's forelimb has become shortened and flattened to make a broad paddle. The arm bones – the humerus, radius and ulna – are very short and the fingers are joined in a common bag of skin. There are five fingers in each flipper, the same number as in the basic vertebrate hand or foot, but three of the fingers are very long. All movement of the arm and hand joints is lost and the flipper has become a rigid structure that articulates only at the shoulder joint, although the whole limb bends under water pressure when used for manœuvring the whale.

A rudimentary hindlimb appears in an embryo whale but it disappears long before the whale is born. All that is left of the hindlimbs and the hips are one or two bones on each side of the body. They are no longer attached to the backbone, as in most mammals, but are buried in a mass of muscle. In males, these bones form an anchor for the penis. The role of locomotion has been taken over by the tail which is thick and powerful, as in fishes. The tip of the tail is drawn out into two flat flukes which act as propellor blades. They are set horizontally and beat up and down, in contrast to those of fishes which are vertical and swing from side to side.

The description given above is of a generalized, anonymous whale but there are many species of whale and they vary considerably in appearance and habits. There is also some confusion about what species can be properly called whales, as distinct from porpoises and dolphins. This has happened because the names of these animals arose centuries before zoologists started to classify animals. It was quite easy to define whales as mammals and not fish but there is still no agreement as to which should be true whales.

Linnaeus grouped the whales, porpoises and dolphins in the order Cetacea and sometimes the whole order is called 'the whales' for convenience. In common language, however, the term 'whale' is usually reserved for the larger members of the order but where the boundary should be drawn is largely a matter of personal preference. One writer may decide that a length of over 6 metres is the qualification of a whale and another may decide on 9 metres or more, but there is always the awkward situation caused by the killer whale. This species sometimes tops 9 metres and is a member of the dolphin family. On the other hand, the pigmy sperm whale, a close relative of the giant sperm whale, reaches only 3·7 metres in length. The white whale or beluga grows to about 4·3 metres and pilot whales 5 metres. Perhaps it is best to describe whales as the 'larger cetaceans'. This vague term describes the animals that form the subject of this book. It is a purely arbitrary

TABLE I

	Probable maximum length (metres)	Distribution
ORDER Cetacea		
SUBORDER Mysticeti (whalebone or baleen whales)		
FAMILY Balaenidae		
Greenland right whale or bowhead (*Balaena mysticetus*)	18	Arctic seas
Biscayan or black right whale (*Eubalaena glacialis*)	ca 18	Cosmopolitan except tropics
Pigmy right whale (*Caperea marginata*)	ca 6	Antarctic seas
FAMILY Eschrichtiidae		
Gray whale (*Eschrichtius robustus*)	ca 14	North Pacific
FAMILY Balaenopteridae (rorquals)		
Blue whale (*Balaenoptera musculus*)	33.3	Cosmopolitan
Fin whale (*B. physalus*)	26	Cosmopolitan
Sei whale (*B. borealis*)	18	Cosmopolitan
Bryde's whale (*B. edeni*)	ca 15	Warmer seas
Minke whale (*B. acutorostrata*)	ca 9.75	Cosmopolitan
Humpback whale (*Megaptera novaeangliae*)	15	Cosmopolitan
SUBORDER Odontoceti (toothed whales)		
FAMILY Physeteridae		
Sperm whale (*Physeter catodon*)	18	Cosmopolitan
Pigmy sperm whale (*Kogia breviceps*)	3.7	Cosmopolitan
Dwarf sperm whale (*K. simus*)	3	Tropics
FAMILY Ziphiidae (beaked whales)		
Baird's beaked whale (*Berardius bairdii*)	13	North Pacific
Arctic bottlenose whale (*Hyperoodon ampullatus*)	ca 9	Arctic seas
Antarctic bottlenose whale (*H. planifrons*)		
FAMILY Delphinidae (dolphins)		
Common pilot whale (*Globicephala melaena*)	ca 7	Cooler seas
Short-finned pilot whale (*G. macrorhyncha*)	ca 6	Warmer seas
Killer whale (*Orcinus orca*)	10	Cosmopolitan

Note: Few specimens of whales have been measured in relation to the numbers caught so larger figures are possible, especially in little-known species. Average lengths of whales caught are much less, about six metres less for the blue whale.

distinction which covers the species that make up the basis of the major whaling industries but which excludes the numerous porpoises and dolphins.

The order Cetacea is divided into two very distinctive sub-orders, the Mysticeti and the Odontoceti, both of which include whales as they are defined above. Most of the true whales are in the Mysticeti, the whalebone or baleen whales. These are the whales which feed mainly on small animals which they sieve from the sea by means of two rows of whalebone or baleen plates hanging from the roof of the mouth. They have no teeth except in the developing embryo. To accommodate the baleen the head is very large and the lower jaw is slightly longer than the upper jaw. With the exception of the sperm whale in the Odontoceti, the whalebone whales have been the whales most sought after by hunters. They are divided into three families.

All members of the family Balaenidae are now rare. They are the right whales, so-called because they were the right whales to catch from open boats. They swim slowly, float when dead and gave large quantities of valuable whalebone. The Biscayan or black right whale became scarce many years ago. It is found in all temperate and sub-polar seas, and the southern form, the southern right whale, is sometimes classed as a separate species. The Greenland right whale or bowhead is confined to Arctic seas.

The right whales are the most distinctive of all whalebone whales. The head takes up one third of the body length. The upper jaw is arched and the lips of the lower jaw rise each side to enclose the numerous baleen plates which grow up to 3·7 metres long. The Biscayan right whale bears a peculiar structure of tough, roughened skin on the snout. This is called the bonnet and has no known function. The bonnet and similar outgrowths around the head are infested with the whale louse, an amphipod crustacean, which lives in the crevices of the horny skin on which it feeds. A similar whale louse lives on the head and flippers of the bowhead.

The pigmy right whale is one of the rarest of whales. It is known almost entirely from specimens stranded on the shores of southern seas and grows to about 5·8 metres, one third the size of the other right whales. It differs from the others in the possession of a dorsal fin.

The right whales are now so rare that sightings are lucky events. There is a small population of bowheads in the North Pacific which is still hunted by Eskimos. Black right whales are extremely rare in the North Atlantic and North Pacific but they are recovering in the southern hemisphere. Prospects are much more encouraging for the gray whale, the sole member of the family Eschrichtiidae. This whale lives on both sides of the North Pacific and was killed in large numbers by the whalers of the nineteenth century. Under strict protection the American population which was two hundred and fifty in 1947 has levelled out at 11,000. Its habit of migrating close to the shores of California, which once made it easy to hunt, has now made it a tourist attraction. Gray whales used to live in the North Atlantic but were hunted to extinction during historical times (see Chapter 8). The gray whale grows to about 4·6 metres. Like the right whales it has no dorsal fin but it has a row of knobs on the back and two or four grooves on the throat, similar to those found on the third family, the Balaenopteridae or rorquals.

The name rorqual is derived from the old Norwegian *rörhval*, referring to the grooves that run from just behind the lower lip to the chest. There is a dorsal fin and the flippers are pointed rather than rounded as in the right whales. Rorquals are more streamlined than the right whales, with flatter heads and short baleen plates. There are six species and among them are the largest of the whales which have formed the mainstay of the whaling industry throughout this century.

The largest of the rorquals is the blue whale, the biggest animal ever to exist. A few specimens have topped 30 metres and the record stands at 33·32 metres for a female. The largest male recorded is 0·6 metres shorter. The weight of such animals is thought to be 130–150 tonnes, much depending on the amount of blubber. Naturally, such giants were eagerly sought by whalers and during the course of this century blue whale numbers have been reduced from an estimated 200,000 to seven or eight thousand. They are now protected and they are recovering slightly. The blue whale was called the 'sulphur-bottom' by whalers because the blue-grey of its belly is sometimes coloured yellow by a film of diatoms.

Small mature blue whales have been caught from time to

time in the Antarctic whaling grounds, particularly around the island of Kerguelen. Some whale authorities consider that these are a race or species of pigmy blue whale but others are sceptical. They feel that this is an attempt to find an excuse to hunt members of a species that has otherwise been given complete protection from hunting.

The second-largest rorqual is the fin whale which reaches about 24 metres. It is the most abundant of the large whales and became the main target of the whalers after the decline of the blue whale. Fin whales look like small, slender blue whales but have larger dorsal fins and white bellies. There is also a strange lop-sided coloration of the head; the lower right lip and the anterior, right-hand baleen plates are white.

Smaller still is the sei (pronounced 'sigh') whale. Seje is the Norwegian for the coalfish, a relative of the cod, and the sei whale appears off parts of the Norwegian coast at the same time each year as the fish. The sei whale looks like the fin whale but only grows to about 18 metres and lacks the asymmetric colouring. Very similar to it is Bryde's (pronounced 'Breuder's) whale, which was distinguished as a separate species only in 1913 and is confined to warmer seas. It is recognized by broader baleen plates, longer ventral grooves which reach as far as the umbilicus and three parallel ridges on the snout. The smallest rorqual is the minke whale or lesser rorqual. It rarely exceeds 9 metres and is recognized by white baleen and a white band on the flippers, which is usually absent in the southern hemisphere. The lesser rorqual earned the name of minke whale when a Norwegian whaler, Miencke, mistook these diminutive rorquals for blue whales.

The last of the rorquals is the humpback whale. Its appearance is very different from the others. The body is stout and the long, narrow flippers measure one third of the total length, whence the scientific name of Megaptera – huge-winged. Both head and flippers are covered with irregular knobs. The ventral grooves are deeper but fewer in number than in other rorquals. The humpback migrates close to the shore so that the routes are well known, but this habit also makes it easy to catch. The numbers of humpbacks were severely reduced but they are slowly increasing under protection.

The second great group of whales is the suborder Odontoceti

or toothed whales. It includes the sperm whale, the killer whale and numerous porpoises and dolphins, many of which are becoming familiar as performing animals in marine aquaria. The jaws of toothed whales are armed with peg teeth, rather like the canines of a dog, and they are used in the capture of fish and squid. The nostrils are combined into a single orifice and there is a rounded forehead, called the melon from the French for a bowler hat. The melon is filled with a fine waxy oil which is a very superior lubricant. The skulls of odontocetes are most unusual in that they are asymmetrical, that is, the left- and right-hand sides are not equal. In some species this has led to the blowhole being on the left side of the head; but asymmetry is most marked in the narwhal where the tusk of the male is a very much enlarged tooth from the left-hand side of the jaw.

The sperm whale or cachalot is the largest of the toothed whales and the most bizarre in appearance. The melon has been enlarged into an enormous, rounded snout of fibrous tissue. The upper part is known as the case and is filled with a clear liquid, called spermaceti, which sets to a wax when cool. Between the case and the jaw is a layer of fibrous fatty tissue called junk by the whalers. The blowhole is at the tip of the snout and to one side rather than on the top of the head. The dorsal fin is replaced by a low hump. Sperm whales were very important commercially in the eighteenth and nineteenth centuries and have become important again as the numbers of rorquals have diminished.

Sperm whales dive to great depths in search of food, which includes giant squid. They live in schools but old males may be solitary. Males grow to twice the size of females, that is to about 18 metres. The most famous sperm whale is Moby Dick, a white 'rogue male'. Although a fictitious character, he was based on stories of rogue males who were well known to whalers. Albinos of the sperm whales and other species have been known to exist and a 16·75 metre white sperm whale, complete with crooked jaw, was caught in the Pacific in 1951, and another of 10·67 metres off Japan in 1957.

The pigmy sperm whale which grows to no more than 3·7 metres, and the dwarf sperm whale a metre smaller, look more like porpoises than their large relatives. Very little is known about them.

Among the larger toothed whales are the bottlenosed and beaked whales of the family Ziphiidae, some of which are extremely rare. Baird's beaked whale reaches 12·8 metres and is hunted in the North Pacific and the two bottlenose whales, one in the Arctic and North Atlantic and the other in the southern hemisphere, grow up to 9 metres. They lack teeth completely except in old males where one tooth erupts on each side of the lower jaw. The Arctic species is hunted.

The two species of pilot whales or blackfish are 6-7 metre dolphins that live in schools sometimes numbering hundreds. For centuries they have been caught in the Faeroes and elsewhere by being driven ashore and stranded. The old name of pothead and the scientific name *Globicephala* refer to the large, rounded melon.

The killer whale is another large dolphin, distinguished by a white patch behind the eye and a tall dorsal fin which reaches 2 metres in old males. The blade-shaped fin led to their being given the confusing name of swordfish (as in the extract from the handbill). The oldest male killer whales grow to more than 9 metres, but females never reach more than half this length. Killer whales live in small groups and feed mainly on fish but they also kill seals and other whales. They, in turn, are hunted to protect fisheries or for their meat and blubber.

2 | The Study of Whales

DURING the Middle Ages, zoology became an armchair study. Animals and their habits were described from previous accounts and from travellers' tales. Not surprisingly, some strange notions crept in, either through faulty recollection or misunderstanding or through attempting to describe what the writer, often a cloistered monk, felt ought to be the way of things. One idea current during this period was that all land animals had their equivalent in the sea, so sea-horses, sea-cows and sea-lions were invented. It is more by good luck than anything else that suitable animals have been found to take these names (the original sea-horses were walruses, not the peculiar little fishes that now bear this name).

There were some strange ideas about whales although at this time they were common around European coasts and not infrequently became stranded. Their large size, strange appearance and marine way of life brought them into the folklore of the seafaring peoples of north-west Europe. Stranded whales were regarded as portents of great events, such as the outbreak of war, and there were good whales that helped with the fishing and bad whales that upset boats and ate men.

Aristotle had, centuries previously, described the main features of whales but his knowledge was ignored until the revival of learning that marked the end of the Middle Ages. Anatomists now took the trouble to dissect stranded specimens (and it was a trouble; witness Buckland's account of the fate that nearly befell an anatomist, quoted in the preceding chapter). Studies of whales at large were much rarer and until the twentieth century there were only two outstanding works devoted to the lives of whales. There was William Scoresby's *Account of the Arctic Regions, with a History and Description of the Northern Whale-fishery*, from which we obtain much of our knowledge of the Greenland right whale, and Charles

Scammon's *The Marine Mammals of the North-western Coasts of North America*, which has a very detailed account of the gray whale.

Apart from the whalers, who generally observed whales in a disturbed situation, to say the least, it was difficult for anyone to study the lives of whales because most of them live in very remote places and they spend much of their time underwater. However, with the great development of whaling in the twentieth century, when it became necessary to find out where the whales were and how they could best be exploited, Government-sponsored research organizations were set up.

Research followed two interrelated courses: the basic study of whale biology and the assessment of the stock of whales with a view to regulating the numbers caught. Neither task was simple because of the scale involved. Dissection of a gigantic whale carcase is not easy, particularly when it causes a delay in the working of the whale factory, and information about the movements of whales and their food supply had to be gathered over a vast area of ocean. Only in the last two decades, as both large whales and the whaling industry appear to be nearing extinction, has it become possible to describe the basic biological facts of population size, growth rate and expectation of life.

The initiative for whale research came from Norway and Britain, originally the two important whaling countries. Pioneer work was started before World War One and was resumed on a large scale afterwards. Emphasis was placed very definitely on the Antarctic populations of whales because they formed the major part of the world's catch. Thus any discussion of whales, their reproduction, feeding or migration, or of whaling, its success or control, is biassed towards the Antarctic and it is quite easy to get the impression that whales and whaling are confined to Antarctic seas. Both are cosmopolitan.

In Norway, whale research took the form of the collection of data from the whaling industry. The Norwegian Whaling Association gathered information about each whale caught: its species, sex, length and the region in which it was caught. This work still continues and the data are published in the *International Whaling Statistics*. Analyses of these figures have given important information about the distribution of whales and their populations.

British research work was directed at the whales themselves, as zoologists were stationed at the whaling factories where they could examine and dissect the whale carcases as they were brought in. The work was directed by the Discovery Committee, a body set up in 1924 to investigate the biology and oceanography of the Falkland Island Dependencies, a large slice of the Southern Ocean and South Atlantic which then enclosed the main Antarctic whaling grounds. The Discovery Committee's work was focussed on whale biology, but the cruises of the *Discovery*, Captain Scott's old expedition ship, and later of the *Discovery II*, were also concerned with other aspects of Antarctic biology and oceanography. With the expansion of the whaling industry to cover all the Southern Ocean, the cruises of the *Discovery II* were extended around the Antarctic continent and the Southern Ocean became the best studied of all oceans.

Observations from the *Discovery* cruises made it possible to plot the distribution of the whales around the Antarctic and to show that concentrations of whales coincided with regions of abundant plankton, the minute floating life of the sea, and that these, in turn, were correlated with movements of ocean currents. This information is of great importance to the whalers who can attempt to forecast the whereabouts of plentiful whales by examination of water temperatures, currents and plankton concentrations.

While the *Discovery* cruises were in progress other zoologists examined over 1,600 whale carcases brought in to whaling factories. Their work formed the basis of much of subsequent whale research. They were able to gather information on the growth and reproduction of whales that was not available from the figures given to the Norwegian statisticians. By examination of their reproductive state throughout the year, the mating season, period of gestation and of suckling were worked out and examination of scars on the ovaries gave the indication of the numbers of calves that had been born.

The extension of this work was to find out the rate of growth, the age of puberty and life expectancy. Such information is essential for working out the structure of the population (the numbers of animals of various ages) and the rate at which new individuals are added to it through breeding. From this it is possible to calculate the rate at which animals can be removed from a population without a serious decrease in numbers. As it was apparent that whaling was causing a decline in the whale populations, it became very important to calculate the breeding rates of the various whale species, so that limits could be placed on the numbers caught. This was impossible until a method of determining the age of a whale had been discovered, so that the information about its reproductive state could be put into perspective.

To determine the age of an animal it is necessary to find some physiological feature that varies with age in a regular fashion. Body length is an obvious choice, but mammals stop growing after they are physically mature and the rate of growth varies between individuals, as is obvious in human beings. What was needed was some feature of the whale that continued growing after maturity and showed a seasonal change in the rate of growth. In other words, the search was for the equivalent of the rings in a tree trunk, each of which represents a year's growth. There seemed to be a good chance that this was possible because the rorqual whales have an annual cycle of feeding in the polar regions during the summer, then migrating to warmer regions to give birth to their young.

The breeding cycle of females was the first seasonal change to be examined. It was found from the dissections made by the Discovery zoologists that the ovaries of whales bore scars, called *corpora albicantia*, and that each one represented an ovulation, the liberation of an egg. In most mammals these scars gradually disappear but they persist in rorquals. By counting the scars on the ovaries of whales the number of ovulations can be determined but the problem was to find out how often a whale ovulated. If once a year, then the age of the whale equalled the number of scars plus the number of years from birth to puberty. If the egg is fertilized, a scar is larger than one from a sterile ovulation, so examination of the ovary gives extra information on how many calves the female bore. The information from corpora albicantia is not wholly accurate but it is useful for assigning relative ages to female whales so that average ages of different populations, or variations in average age, can be determined.

Ovary scars can, of course, be found only in females but

there are two characters common to both sexes of rorquals which continue to grow throughout life. Baleen plates grow continuously from the roof of the mouth and each one is inscribed with irregular ridges that represent variations in the rate of growth. Unfortunately, like fingernails, the continuous growth of baleen plates is balanced by the wearing away of the tip so that only a few ridges are present in older whales. There are normally no more than four ridges visible but counting them is a means of ageing young whales and has allowed the age of puberty to be determined.

The best method so far found for calculating the age of a whale was discovered by P. E. Purves while he was studying the mechanism of hearing. Blocking the outer passage of the ear is a long, horny 'plug' which conducts sound to the ear-drum (see Chapter 4). When cut down the middle, each earplug reveals a series of growth layers where material has been laid down. These layers or laminae are found in both sexes and do not get worn away so they appear to be perfect indicators of age. The difficulty was, once again, to find the rate at which the laminae are laid down. They could be formed annually, or biennially perhaps, depending on what physiological changes control the laying down of the horny material. Proof that the laminae were laid down annually came from examination of whales caught before and after the summer feeding. This showed that the structure of each lamina is related to the annual cycle of feeding and fasting. Detailed examination revealed that the second lamina of each plug is the broadest and corresponds to the rapid growth during suckling. Thereafter, the laminae become narrower as the growth slows and, very conveniently for whale biologists, the laminae are irregular until puberty, when they start to be laid down evenly.

The problem with finding methods of age determination in all animals is to mark them when very young so that animals of known age can be obtained in later years and the methods of age determination checked accurately. In some groups of animals this has been quite easy. Birds are conveniently marked by placing a numbered ring on the leg; fish are tagged with discs pinned to their bodies; and land mammals have their ears clipped or tagged. None of these methods can be used for whales, nor can branding which has been used on seals.

The inspiration for the modern method of marking whales which is now used with considerable success lies in accidental discoveries from the days of hand-harpooning. It was not unusual for a whale to get away with a harpoon – or more than one – stuck in its back. Years later, perhaps, it would be successfully harpooned. The old harpoon heads, still identifiable, were found in its flesh and showed where the first attack had been made. Systematic marking of whales started in the 1920s when the Discovery Committee scientists tried firing marks like outsize barbed drawing pins into the backs of whales. The idea was for the marks to be clearly visible, but they fell out too easily. The next step was to shoot aluminium, and later stainless steel, darts from a special 12-bore gun. The dart bore a number, the address of the Discovery Committee and the promise of a £1 reward if the mark and details of its discovery were sent in.

The method was a success, so marking became a practical proposition and, between 1926 and 1939, 5,350 whales were marked by Discovery expeditions, mainly from the *William Scoresby*, a small ship built on the lines of a whale-catcher. The use of a ship for whale-marking is very expensive but since World War Two, some eight nations have marked whales from special ships, whale-catchers or from helicopters.

Marking with darts has one great drawback. To lodge securely the dart has to penetrate deep into the muscles of the back. This means that it is unlikely to be discovered until the whale is almost dismembered at the factory, by which time much vital material, such as the ear plugs and ovaries, may be lost. Worse still, the dart may be missed completely and only discovered when the meat boilers are cleaned out. By this time it will be impossible to tell from which whale it came. Nevertheless, marking has yielded results. Of the 4,988 whales marked by Discovery Committee ships, 396 had been recovered from blue, fin and humpback whales by 1974. Since 1945 there have been international marking programmes covering most of the whaling grounds. Over 20,000 have been tagged and, in the Southern Ocean, nearly fifteen per cent have been recovered.

The results from marking programmes have not been particularly helpful in the problem of ageing whales. This is because it is impossible to find out much about a whale at the time that the dart is inserted. There will be no indication of its age unless it is a calf. Marking calves has the drawback of the danger of a dart causing severe wounds, but humpback calves have been tagged successfully. More useful information has been gathered about the migrations of whales which show whales from one summer feeding ground migrate to a particular breeding area in winter and that a group from one area often keeps separate from other groups.

Unfortunately the recovery of a mark does not tell us where a whale went and what it did between marking and capture. One blue whale was caught 3,000 kilometres from the place of marking after an interval of fifty-seven days. What is not known is whether it swam in a straight line between the two points, whether it cruised evenly at fifty-three kilometres per day and fed as it travelled, or whether the 3,000 kilometres was covered in only a fraction of the fifty-seven days.

A new alternative to marking is to identify individuals by the pattern of the body coloration. For instance, humpbacks have white patches on the underside of the flukes, which they show off as they dive. Each whale appears to have a unique pattern of patches, so their movements and habits can be studied without molesting them.

After World War Two, when whaling was resumed again after an almost complete lapse of several years, several countries joined Norway and Britain in promoting the research into whale biology. Both scope and scale of the research have increased in consequence. It is now possible to estimate the numbers of most whale species, and it is abundantly clear that they have been seriously reduced from their former numbers. It is also possible to estimate the rate at which baby whales are born into a population and therefore the rate at which a species can be hunted or at which it will recover if hunting is checked, although the precise figures for particular populations may be disputed by different authorities.

Longevity, numbers and birth rate are the practical problem of whale biology which need to be answered if whales are to survive but there is also an increasing interest by zoologists

1. The replica of an eighty-foot blue whale. It is based on a carcase of a whale caught off Norway

2. Section of the earplug of a baleen whale, showing the growth lines

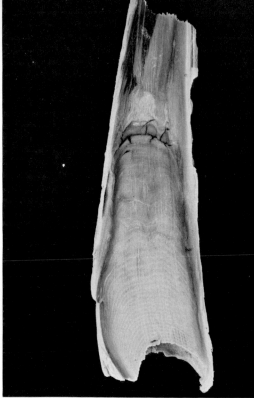

3. The fibrous ends of whalebone form a sieve on each side of the long, narrow palate

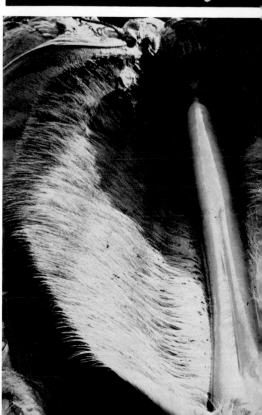

in the behaviour of whales: their courtship and family life, and their ability to dive to great depths, locate food and navigate in the vast volume of the sea. The large cetaceans do not lend themselves easily to such studies and the bulk of our knowledge of cetacean behaviour comes from observations on the dolphins and smaller specimens of the great whales which are kept in marine aquaria. For the whales, information used to come from the whalers and from observant crewmen of merchant and naval vessels. When gathered together such accounts can give some inkling about the habits of the giants of the animal world, and to some extent it is allowable to use the studies on captive dolphins to draw conclusions about the behaviour of whales. The situation is now changing as ways are sought for observing whales at close quarters in the wild. This is more difficult than formerly because there are fewer whales to watch, but close-up work by SCUBA divers and long distance observation from aircraft is opening a window on whales' lives.

3 | Life at Sea

FOUR groups of mammals have taken to the sea: the carnivores, seals, sirenians and whales. The carnivores have only one representative, the sea otter which spends virtually its entire life at sea. Apart from a few living in fresh waters the seals of the order Pinnipedia are marine but, although beautifully adapted for swimming and able to search for food in deep water, they betray their terrestrial ancestry by the retention of the hindlimbs as flippers. The fur seals and sea lions turn their hindlimbs forward and lift the body clear of the ground when bounding along the shore. The true seals, which include the Common and Grey seals of European coasts, cannot do this and have to move on land by hitching their bodies along like giant caterpillars. Nevertheless all seals come out of the water, onto land or ice floes, to give birth.

The third group, the manatees and the dugong of the order Sirenia, are superficially like the whales in appearance. The skin is hairless, the forelimbs are paddle-shaped, the hindlimbs are missing and the tail is expanded horizontally into flukes. Sirenians rarely, if ever, come ashore and the young are born in the water. Their ribs are weak so that their lungs would be squashed by the weight of the body on land, and the skin cracks if it is allowed to dry out. Yet, although the sirenians spend their whole lives in the water, they do not seem to be as fully aquatic as even the seals. They stay near the shore in calm water and cannot remain underwater for long.

The cetaceans alone have completely conquered the sea and have cut free from the land fully to colonize the oceans. They can be considered a very successful group of animals in both their abundance and diversity and this may be due to the lack of competition with other mammals once they left the land. A whole new world opened to them which, during the course of their evolution, they have exploited in two main ways. One group, the whalebone whales, became specialized for feeding on the swarms of small floating animals. The abundance of this food allowed them to develop body sizes that are impossible to attain on land. The other group, the toothed whales, became carnivores, feeding mainly on fish and squid. Except for the sperm whale, the toothed whales do not approach the whalebone whales in size but they have made up for this in diversity. The dolphins, the pigmies among cetaceans, do not concern us here but the fifty-odd species are to be found out at sea, inshore and even far up rivers and in lakes.

The first requirement of an aquatic animal is the ability to swim and it is to this end that a whale's body is organized. The body of a whale is very fish-like and its method of swimming also bears a close resemblance to the movements of fishes. The flippers of a whale and the pectoral fins of a fish are used mainly for steering and balance. The propulsive effort comes from the beating of the tail whose power is transmitted to the water by the broad surfaces of the flukes or tail fins.

The trunk of the whale's body is very rigid but the tail is flexible and is hinged at its point of attachment to the lumbar region of the back, at the region of the vestigial pelvis. The lumbar region is the powerhouse of the whale and contains massive muscles which are attached by long tendons to the vertebrae in the tail. These muscles contract rhythmically to raise and lower the tail stock, which is flattened from side to side to reduce resistance to its up and down movement through the water. The power generated in the lumbar muscles and tail is released through the flukes, flat blades of tough fibres that pivot at the tip of the tail. The main propulsive effort comes on the 'upstroke' and the flukes are held so that they force water backwards and the whale forward. The downstroke is a recovery stroke and the flukes bend passively to reduce resistance. The tail can also swing sideways to alter the direction of the thrust so that the whale is power-steered, like a boat with an outboard motor.

The work of the propulsive unit is made easier by the streamlining of the body, which is shaped like the fuselage of an aeroplane, with a pointed nose and tapering towards the rear. Any projections, like ears, are reduced to a minimum or eliminated, although the dorsal fin, which acts as a stabilizer, is largest in the fastest species. The skin is very smooth and virtually hairless although whales can be fouled by barnacles and other clinging animals in the same way as the hull of a ship. One humpback whale was found to have 450 kg of barnacles adhering to it and it is said that humpbacks migrating up the west coast of Africa will move towards the coast where the Congo River flows into the sea and the relatively fresh water will kill off their barnacles. It is also said that sailing vessels used to be brought there for the same purpose.

Dolphins can swim at high speed because the water flows evenly over the surface of the body without breaking into eddies of turbulence. Turbulence creates drag and its replacement by smooth 'laminar flow' reduces the drag on a dolphin's body by ninety per cent. It appears that dolphins can eliminate turbulence by their elastic skins forming gentle folds which match variations in the waterflow. Presumably the great whales are similarly equipped to slide through the water with the minimum of disturbance.

The power produced by the large rorquals is immense. They can leap clear of the water and, when harpooned, tow catcher boats weighing several hundred tons. There is a record of a blue whale towing a whale-catcher, with its engines running full astern, at 11 kph for several hours. *The Guinness Book of Animal Facts and Feats* comments that this must be the ultimate in animal power. It must also be the record for the tensile strength of rope.

The maximum speed that whales can attain is not easy to measure, particularly as there is a difference between the short burst of a sprinter and the steady pace of a long-distance runner. Under natural conditions whales have little need to move at more than a steady pace, although the toothed whales need to dash after their prey. The right whales are the dawdlers among whales, cruising at 3–8 kph and making 16 kph over short distances when chased. Humpbacks are also slow movers but the sperm whale averages 16 kph with short bursts of up to 32 kph. Rorquals are the fastest, as well as the largest, whales and even modern motor whale-catchers cannot catch up with them without effort. The cruising speed of blue and fin whales is about 19 kph but they can sustain up to 24 kph for a couple of hours, and reach 48 kph or more over very short distances. The fastest whale is the slender sei whale which has been reported as reaching 56 kph for a very short time.

Very occasionally some whales will leap clear of the sea, apparently for fun, but as a general rule they come to the surface only to breathe or 'blow'. The minimum possible time is spent changing the air in the lungs and very little of the body is exposed during the process. As little as two or three seconds are spent in blowing, but a part of the whale is visible for another four or five seconds as its head goes down and its back rises then slips out of view. Within this short space of time, the whale has to empty and refill its lungs. Although they are comparatively small, a larger proportion of the air in the lungs is exchanged when compared with land mammals. Only fifteen per cent of the air in human lungs is exchanged at each breath but the whale discharges eighty-five to ninety per cent of its lung volume. This is around 1,100 litres, which accounts for the explosive 'whoosh' of a whale's blow as air rushes out at nearly 500 kph.

Several blows follow in quick succession after which the whale dives or 'sounds' and is not seen for a good few minutes. Sperm or humpback whales flip their flukes out of the water before finally disappearing, leaving a round slick on the water. Rorquals stay under for five to ten minutes but the sperm whale usually stays under for twenty minutes. The duration of a sound depends on what the whale is doing; whether it is feeding, cruising slowly or hurrying. A resting fin whale blows once or twice a minute but, when whales are pursued and are fleeing at speed, they have to blow more frequently and after a very prolonged dive a whale has to lie panting at the surface.

Each time a whale blows a characteristic plume of vapour bursts from its blowhole. In medieval pictures this was depicted as a fountain of water and whales were said to spout. While the blow is definitely not a jet of water, it is likely that water still swilling around the blowhole is sprayed up by the rush of air. The main reason for the blow is the condensation of vapour in the breath, such as we produce on a cold day when our warm humid breath mingles with cold air. That the blow is still visible in the tropics is due to the cooling of the air as it rushes out. A gas cools if pressure is released, in a process known as adiabatic expansion. This is the principle behind the working of a refrigerator and it can be experienced when fizzy drinks are made with a 'sparklet' bulb. The explosive release of carbon dioxide from the bulb cools the surrounding metal. In the whale's blow cooling causes condensation of water vapour. Additional spray may come from water and oil from the breathing passages. The ears of whales are surrounded by airsacs which connect with the windpipe. The airsacs are filled with an oily foam which is secreted from glands. It is thought possible that some of this foam is sucked out at each blow with the rush of air and hangs in the air as a fine cloud. Whatever the cause, it is the blow that is the first, and often only, sight that we get of a whale. Depending on conditions the blow may rise for 6 metres and hang for a few seconds before dispersing. With experience this is sufficient to identify a whale. Right whales can be distinguished by a double, V-shaped blow, rorquals have a single blow and the blow of sperm whales rises at a steep angle rather than vertically (Figure 2).

Figure 2 From left to right, the blows of a right whale, a fin whale and a sperm whale.

The blubber surrounding the whale's body acts as a very necessary insulation to keep in heat. It is necessary not only in freezing polar waters. Even in the tropics the sea temperature is still much lower than the body temperature of warm-blooded animals, and water temperature nearly always decreases with depth. Heat is also lost during respiration but this is less important in slow-breathing cetaceans than in land mammals, which are pumping out hot air many times a minute. However, the blubber would make a fast-swimming whale as uncomfortable as an athlete sprinting in an overcoat if it did not have the means of getting rid of the heat generated in the massive blocks of muscle. The heat is removed from the muscles by the circulating blood and is carried to the surface of the body, where it is lost into the water. If body heat has to be conserved, perhaps when the whale is resting in polar seas, circulation to the periphery of the body is reduced and heat loss is cut.

The thin, blubber-free flippers, fin and flukes present a large surface for the loss of heat and act as radiators. This is very useful when the whale is overheating but could be disastrous when heat needs to be conserved. Blood flow to these organs cannot be cut off completely but heat loss is virtually eliminated by a common engineering device: the heat exchanger. The arteries within the flippers, fin or fluke have a ring of smaller veins closely adhering along their length. As hot blood flows down the artery its heat is absorbed by the cool blood returning in the veins. This is called a countercurrent heat exchanger and it works efficiently because, as the arterial blood gives up its heat, it is always meeting cooler venous blood so there is an outward flow of heat along the length of the artery in the countercurrent system. Thus, heat carried by the blood out of the main bulk of the body is immediately picked up and carried back in before it can be lost to the sea. During exercise, the countercurrent system is by-passed, the radiator comes into action and body heat is lost.

Although so little is seen of whales, they live not far beneath the surface of the sea, at depths where sunlight still penetrates. The small floating animals on which whalebone whales feed are most abundant in the top ten metres of the sea and it is rare for these whales to go farther down. The toothed whales, on the other hand, and sperm whales in particular, need to descend to greater depths in search of fish and squid.

The depths reached by sperm whales during their regular dives are not known but these whales have been found entangled in submarine cables. The record is held by the recovery of a sperm whale skeleton from a cable lying on the sea bed at 1,134 metres. It is assumed that the whale was feeding when its jaw became entangled in the cable. There is circumstantial evidence for deeper diving when two sperm whales were watched diving for food from a spotter plane. The whales were soon caught and *Scymodon* sharks were found in their stomachs. These sharks are found only on the sea bed, which was over 3,000 metres deep in this area. A harpooned fin whale has dived to five hundred metres but rorquals do not normally go below one hundred metres. Records for duration of dives also come from harpooned animals. A sperm whale stayed under for seventy-five minutes and a blue whale for forty-nine minutes.

The ability of whales, and other marine animals, to dive to such depths raises several questions about physiological adaptation. Even with self-contained underwater breathing apparatus (SCUBA) a human diver has difficulty descending to depths of fifty metres or more because of the incredible pressure that is exerted by the weight of water as he goes down. For each ten metres of the descent the pressure increases by one atmosphere (about one kilogram per square centimetre) so that a deep-diving sperm whale encounters pressures of one hundred atmospheres or one hundred kilograms per square centimetre. To prevent the lungs being flooded by water forced into the air passages and lungs, the blowhole is kept watertight by powerful elastic lips and in the deep-diving odontocetes there is a system of blocks and valves formed by the airsacs around the nasal passage.

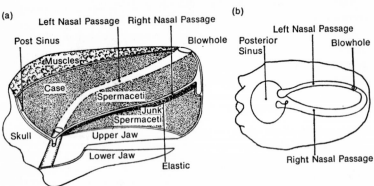

Figure 3 Diagrams of a sperm whale head in (a) side view and (b) top view to show the breathing passages (after Raven and Gregory). Note the single blowhole which is off-centre.

There would also be a danger of water being forced down the windpipe when the odontocete whale feeds if its windpipe were connected to the throat in the same way as in man. We can breathe through the mouth as well as through the nostrils, the two airstreams meeting at the top of the throat to pass into the windpipe. In whales the epiglottis at the top of the windpipe is extended in the form of a 'beak' to fit into the nasal passage, so separating the feeding and breathing routes. This is, however, not essential as whalebone whales and other mammals, including man, can eat and swallow under water with safety. It could be that the 'beak' is important for the toothed whales which feed at great depths and that it also prevents air from escaping through the mouth when water pressure is squeezing the lungs.

One of the great dangers to SCUBA divers is decompression sickness, or the 'bends'. This is caused by breathing air supplied at the same pressure as the surrounding water so that a large amount of nitrogen from the air accumulates in solution in the body. Nitrogen is the main constituent of air and it is not poisonous under normal circumstances but, because it is not in-volved in any of the body's metabolic processes, it remains in the bloodstream and tissues. It does no harm there, but a SCUBA diver breathing under pressure accumulates a large amount of nitrogen in his tissues and when he surfaces, the pressure is released and the nitrogen bubbles out of solution, like the bubbles of carbon dioxide rising from a bottle of tonic water when the cap is removed. Any bubbles of oxygen are soon used up by the body but bubbles of nitrogen persist and are extremely damaging. They collect in the blood vessels where they form painful and sometimes fatal air-locks and, because nitrogen is absorbed particularly by fatty tissues, bubbles are particularly liable to appear in the fatty coverings of nerve fibres where they disrupt the functioning of the nerves and cause paralysis.

The 'bends' are prevented by the diver surfacing slowly so that the pressure is gently relaxed and the nitrogen has time to dissolve out of the blood and be passed out through the lungs. An alternative is for the diver to breathe a gas mixture that does not contain nitrogen. For the whales, the problem hardly exists because they do not breathe compressed air. The risk of the bends is virtually eliminated in the first place because the whales submerge with only the nitrogen contained in one deep breath and it is dissolved in the body fluids at only a fairly low pressure. They do not continue breathing while submerged like a SCUBA diver.

Human breathold divers, going down without breathing apparatus, can get the bends after repeated dives, so there is still some slight danger. However, as the whale descends, increasing pressure on its body flattens the thorax and squeezes the lungs. These collapse so that air is forced out of them into the thick-walled windpipe and bronchial tubes where it cannot be absorbed. The result is that the absorption of nitrogen is reduced until, at one hundred metres, the lungs are collapsed completely and absorption is eliminated. Furthermore, some nitrogen in the air passages and lungs is believed to be absorbed by the oily foam in the complex airsacs and may be blown out in the foam during exhalation (see p. 38).

To be able to survive a long dive (a maximum of over one hour for sperm whales) with only the air contained in the lungs, a careful husbanding of oxygen supplies is essential. A whale's lungs are surprisingly small for the size of its body and they carry only about one tenth of the oxygen stored for use in a dive. A human diver working without diving apparatus, on the other hand, carries a third of his oxygen store in the lungs. In whales a large amount of oxygen is stored in the muscles where it is bound to myoglobin, a substance related to oxygen-carrying haemoglobin in the blood. Like haemoglobin, myoglobin is dark red and the large quantities found in the muscles of diving animals accounts for their almost black meat.

The precious store of oxygen is conserved by the almost complete shut-down of inessential body activities. The heart-beat slows down (from sixty to thirty beats per minute in killer whales) and the blood circulation shuts down except to supply the vital functions of the heart and nervous system.

During the dive the swimming muscles, which must, of course, keep going, function without oxygen. They get their energy from anaerobic respiration. This is the process by which carbohydrates are partially oxidized to lactic acid and energy is released without the use of oxygen. The lactic acid is stored until the whale surfaces. It then pants – 'has its spoutings out' the whalers said – inhaling oxygen to break down the lactic acid to water and carbon dioxide and exhaling the carbon dioxide. A human sprinter does the same thing. During a short burst of speed his lungs cannot supply sufficient oxygen; an 'oxygen debt' is built up and has to be repaid by panting afterwards.

The working of the blood system is one of the aspects of whale biology which is still a mystery. There are several modifications in the structures of the system, as compared with land mammals, but their functions are often not understood. The heart, rather surprisingly, is fairly small but the interesting feature of the blood system is the number of tangled masses of small blood vessels. Called *retia mirabilia*, or 'wonderful networks', the tangles may be made up of arterial or venous vessels, or both. They are found between the ribs, around the spine and at the base of the brain, and around the eyeballs. There have been half a dozen suggestions as to their use: they may be blood reservoirs, expandable space fillers to compensate for pressure effects on the body or they may help to equalize differences in blood pressure during diving. There is no conclusive evidence for any of these possibilities and, as land mammals have *retia mirabilia*, it is not impossible that they are not connected with diving at all. An adaptation of more obvious use is the many large thin-walled veins which must act as reservoirs for blood when the circulation slows down during a dive.

It must be realized that the information a dead whale can supply is limited and much of our knowledge of the body mechanisms in living whales is speculative. It has been possible to measure the heart beat of captive dolphins in marine aquaria but it can only be surmised that the same thing happens in a blue whale. There is much of the physiology of whales that is a mystery or, at least, open to debate. The function of the enormous, bulbous forehead of the sperm whale with its case of spermaceti has been the subject of several theories. M. R. Clarke, considers it possible that the case is acting as a buoyancy tank, an idea not accepted by all authorities.

The theory goes as follows: a sperm whale is just buoyant at the surface and evidence suggests that it can lie still at great depths and so must be neutrally buoyant there, although the density of seawater will have increased. Therefore the sperm whale must reduce its density as it dives and control its buoyancy very carefully. As spermaceti sets from a fluid to a solid wax at around 31° Centigrade (roughly blood heat), Clarke calculates that cooling and warming the spermaceti changes the buoyancy of the whale so that it stays neutrally buoyant at any depth, and it does not have to waste energy in maintaining its depth. When it needs to surface it can come up like a submarine without physical effort, by pumping blood through the capillaries in the case. The spermaceti warms up, becoming less dense and lifting the whale to the surface.

4 | Submarine Senses

LIKE any other animal, a whale needs to be aware of its surroundings, to know the physical conditions of temperature, light and gravity, to know where its fellows are and how to obtain its food. It is able to do this through its sense organs, each of which collects specific information to enable the animal to conduct its activities properly. Man relies principally on sight, with hearing playing an important part and smell, touch and taste filling minor roles. These are the traditional five senses and the relative importance of each is different in various animals. Dogs, for instance, place a great reliance on smell, while bats make use of an acute sense of hearing for their echo-location and can hear high-pitched sounds far beyond the range of our ears.

It is not surprising, therefore, to find that the whales are equipped with senses that are considerably different from ours. Their sense organs have to function underwater and this immediately imposes restrictions on mechanisms which were evolved by terrestrial ancestors living in air. Vision is our main sense but as soon as we dive underwater it becomes obvious that eyesight is of limited use. Even in the clearest water it is impossible to make out objects at a distance greater than about fifteen metres. The turbidity of sea water results in a much lower visibility in practice and visibility wanes rapidly with increasing depth. At ten metres only one tenth of the sunlight remains and at four hundred metres it is pitch dark. Consequently vision can only be of limited use even to whalebone whales feeding near the surface. It is useless for sperm whales diving deep for squid.

There is a second drawback to vision underwater for an animal with eyes designed for use in air. When we swim underwater without the benefit of a facemask our eyes become long-sighted. The focusing power of the eye depends on light being bent as it passes through both the cornea and the lens and adjustments in the lens ensure that images fall on the sensitive retina. In air, the curvature of the lens accounts for only a small part of the total focusing power, the major part being due to refraction at the surface of the cornea as light enters the eye. The bending of light rays at the cornea depends on the difference between the refractive index of the corneal tissue and that of air and on the curvature of the cornea. In other words, the cornea is acting as an extra lens. When underwater, our eyes lose the benefit of corneal refraction because the refractive indices of water and corneal tissue are almost identical and the light is not bent as it passes from one to the other. The only refraction remaining is that at the lens and the result is longsightedness, with the image being formed behind the retina and vision becoming blurred.

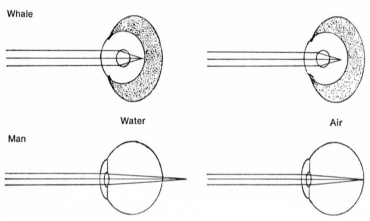

Figure 4 Vision in whales and man. In air a whale's eye becomes shortsighted because light is focused in front of the retina; in water a man's becomes longsighted because light is focused behind the retina.

To compensate for this deficiency, the eye of a whale has an almost spherical lens, for the more curved a lens the greater is its focusing power. Spherical lenses are also found in the eyes of seals and fishes, showing this to be a common solution to the problem. There are other adaptations for a marine environment. Tear glands are unnecessary as the eye is continually bathed in salt water, but to protect it against the wear of the water streaming past, an oily substance is secreted from the corner of the eye and the surface of the cornea is unusually tough. The sclera, or outside coat, of the eyeball is also very thick and tough, and this prevents the eyeball being distorted by pressure changes when the whale dives. To compensate for the dim light, there is the tapetum, a layer of reflective material, lying behind the retina. It is the tapetum that causes a cat's eyes to shine in the dark, its function being to reflect light back to the retina a second time so that the sensitivity of vision is increased.

In general, then, it appears that whales have passably good eyes, but vision must still play a relatively minor role in their lives because of the position of the eyes on the head. Whalers used to approach sperm whales from the front or the back, where the whales could not see them; and a captive pilot whale ignored food placed in front of its snout because it could not see it there. Bottle-nosed dolphins, on the other hand, have their eyes set far enough forward for stereoscopic vision and the excellence of their vision is shown by the feats of captive dolphins leaping clear of their pools to take titbits from their keeper's hand.

Compared with vision, hearing is an excellent sense for a marine animal because sound travels very well through water. So it is not surprising to find that hearing is the whale's most important sense. A human diver cannot hear at all well and completely loses the ability to locate the source of a sound, because human ears are designed for use in air, but the whales have evolved modifications that enable their ears to work efficiently underwater. The changes become clear in a comparison of the structure of a whale's ear with that of a man.

The ear of mammals is divided into outer, middle and inner parts. The outer ear consists of a tube, the meatus, leading into the head and ending at a membrane, the eardrum, which separates it from the middle ear. Around the opening of the meatus is a flap of cartilage, the pinna, which collects sound waves and directs them into the meatus. The waves travel down the meatus and strike the eardrum, setting up vibrations in it which are carried to three small bones, the auditory ossicles. The ossicles lie in the air-filled cavity of the middle ear and hinge together like a series of levers, amplifying the vibrations and transmitting them to the fluid-filled tubes of the inner ear. The inner ear consists of the semicircular canals, the organ of balance and not concerned with hearing, and the cochlea, a spiral tube equipped with a set of sense cells that register vibrations which have come from the middle ear and transmit their message to the brain.

To summarize, the mammalian ear collects vibrations in the air, then amplifies and converts them into vibrations in the fluid of the inner ear so that the sense cells can be stimulated. The mechanism of the whale ear follows the same basic pattern but it is adapted to collect vibrations from water. It also has to function efficiently under great pressures.

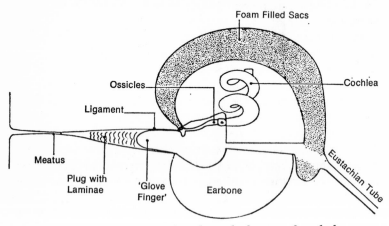

Figure 5 A diagrammatic section through the ear of a whale.

The whale has no earflap or pinna, which would be an obstruction to streamlining, and all that can be seen of the ear is a small slit in the skin which leads to a very narrow meatus. In fin whales and other whalebone whales it is just possible to push a little finger into the meatus but the central part of the meatus is completely closed and is no more than a string of connective tissue. It then opens out again into a narrow tube which runs to the eardrum. This is a more complex structure than the simple drum-like membrane of the human ear. In whalebone whales the membrane of the eardrum is in the form of a taut ligament attached to a ring of bone and an elongated tube like the finger of a glove which lies in the meatus. Fitting over the 'glove finger' and blocking up the meatus is the 'ear plug' of concentric layers of horny material shed from the lining of the meatus which is used in determining the age of whalebone whales (see Chapter 3).

Vibrations in the surrounding water are transmitted down the meatus, the parallel fibres of the connective tissues making up the closed section being a better conductor of sound than the surrounding blubber. The ear plug is also a good sound conductor and it carries sounds to the eardrum and sets the three auditory ossicles in motion. From there onwards, there is little difference between the working of the ears of land mammals and whales except that the ossicles of the whale's ear are arranged to give a greater amplification and provision has to be made for the ear to work under pressure.

For the eardrum and ossicles to vibrate freely it is necessary for the air pressure in the middle ear to have a pressure equal to that of the medium on the outside of the eardrum. In land mammals this is maintained by the eustachian tube, a narrow tube running from the middle ear to the throat. Changes of pressure on the outside of the eardrum are balanced by a valve in the eustachian tube allowing air in or out of the middle ear. An increase in external pressure caused by diving or even driving down a steep hill forces the eardrum in and gives rise to a feeling of discomfort in the ears. We relieve this by 'swallowing' and allowing air to pass up the eustachian tube so that pressure on each side of the eardrum is equalized and the ossicles are allowed to vibrate freely again.

A whale cannot swallow in this manner and its eustachian tubes end in large airsacs surrounding the ears. As the whale dives and the pressure around it increases, the airsacs are squeezed and air is forced into the middle ear to counteract the increased pressure on the eardrum. The constrictive effect of pressure is also counteracted by two muscles attached to the ligament of the eardrum, which contract to equalize the inward movement of the eardrum.

So far it has been explained how the whale ear is adapted to convert sound in water to vibrations of the ossicles in the middle ear and how it can do this despite wide variations in pressure, but the whale still faces the problems that make the human ear inefficient underwater. In a land animal sound waves travel through the air-filled passage of the outer ear and therefore have to pass along the ossicles where they are amplified. Sound waves do not by-pass the eardrum and auditory ossicles because they cannot pass directly from the air to the bone of the skull and so cannot stimulate the sense cells in the cochlea directly. When underwater, the eardrum and ossicles are by-passed because sound travels easily from water into bone and thence directly to the cochlea. The amplifying effect of the ossicles is consequently lost and hearing is impaired.

Conduction of sound through the skull also prevents a human diver from telling the position of a source of sound. The direction of a sound is judged by minute differences in the time taken to reach each ear, or by a minute difference in the loudness in each ear. If a sound comes from a source directly in front of the head, it will reach both ears simultaneously but if the source is moved to the left, the sound will reach the left ear first. The head acts as a barrier so that sound waves have to travel round it to enter the right ear. When underwater sound enters the skull at any point, the head ceases to be a barrier and sound waves travel direct to both ears.

Whales have overcome the difficulty of the conduction of sound from water to bone by a number of devices that isolate the ear mechanism from the skull so that it responds only to sounds passing down the meatus and through the ossicles. The bones that surround the ear are very dense and so hard that it is difficult to saw them without their splintering. The high density prevents them from resonating when the lighter bones of the skull vibrate. Furthermore, these bones are not intimately attached to the skull, as in other mammals, but are loosely attached by connective tissue which does not conduct sound well. The earbones of whales can be wrenched off the skull and they are sometimes found washed up on beaches. The space between these earbones and the skull is filled by the airsacs leading from the eustachian tube. They are filled with an oily foam secreted by glands in their walls which forms another barrier to sound coming through the skull.

It was only in 1960 that F. C. Fraser and P. E. Purves of the

Natural History Museum in London demonstrated these mechanisms and showed that whales hear in exactly the same manner as other mammals but with special adaptations to make this possible. Until this time no one had been able to see how whales had overcome the problem of conduction of sound through bone. The first scientists to write on the subject considered that whales had a poor sense of hearing or that they were deaf even, but their speculations were not based on observations of the behaviour of live animals and they must have been ignorant of whalers' lore. The whalers of the eighteenth and nineteenth centuries knew perfectly well that they had to approach sperm whales very cautiously as the splash of an oar or the thump of a foot against the side of the boat alerted the whales and sent them fleeing.

It is now known from experiments on the hearing of dolphins that they have a sense of hearing second only to that of bats. Bottle-nosed dolphins can hear sounds up to a pitch of 153 kilocycles, compared with an upper limit of 175 kilocycles for bats and a mere twenty kilocycles for man. The upper limit of hearing for whales is not known and, in any case, it is most likely that, as with bats and dolphins, they are most sensitive to sounds within a range somewhat below the upper limit. It is known for instance that whalebone whales are sensitive to asdic which transmits tones of twenty to forty kilocycles. This sensitivity has limited the use of asdic for whale-hunting along the lines of submarine hunting but it has been used in the method of whaling called *prøser jag* in which whales are chased and so forced to surface at short intervals to breathe (see Chapter 12). It is also known that the ears of whales show anatomical features connected with a sensitivity to high tones. The earplug is a particularly good conductor of high tones and one of the ossicles is attached to the middle ear by bony rather than by soft tissue, a condition also found in bats. There is also evidence that the cochlea is particularly sensitive to high tones.

The sensitivity of the whale ear can be demonstrated by anatomical investigation and simple observations such as those described above but it is a much harder task to find out what whales are using their ears for. By analogy with land mammals, it would seem that whales could use their ears for listening for prey and enemies or for communicating with their fellows. A further possibility is that, as their hearing is extremely sensitive, they are, like bats, using a system of echolocation or sonar to find their prey and to detect obstacles in the water.

It is the use of sonar by cetaceans that has received the greatest interest since it has been found that dolphins kept in captivity can avoid swimming into nets even when the water is very murky. The ease of training dolphins to carry out tests under controlled conditions has led to the discovery that they have an extremely sensitive form of sonar. For instance, one dolphin was trained to swim towards the larger of a pair of metal balls suspended in the water while wearing rubber cups over the eyes. It was frequently able to distinguish a 6·35 centimetre sphere from a 5·57 centimetre sphere. Other experiments have shown that dolphins can distinguish the texture of different objects and even discriminate between kinds of fish they like and dislike by means of sonar.

Dolphins locate and identify objects by emitting a stream of extremely powerful, very short clicks. Echoes are reflected from objects in front of the dolphin and picked up and identified. The clicks would be deafening to us except that they are of extremely short duration and, although audible, most of their energy is emitted at very high frequencies (up to 100 kilocycles), well beyond the range of our hearing. The loudness of sperm whale clicks is equivalent to standing six metres behind a jet engine.

The clicks probably originate either in the region of the pharynx, in the wind pipe, or in the passages around the blow-hole; there is no agreement on this. Transmission of the clicks and reception of their echoes is another area of dispute. One suggestion is that the broad 'dish' of the frontal part of the skull acts as a reflector beaming the clicks through the oily melon, the dolphins' equivalent of the sperm whale's spermaceti. The melon acts as a lens focusing the clicks into a narrow beam. Returning echoes are received in the hollow, oil-filled bones of the jaws and carried back to the ears which lie by the jaw hinges. This theory is not accepted by all whale biologists. There is some evidence to support it but there are also objections.

Meanwhile, the story of how cetacean sonar works will have

to remain unsatisfactory and vague. It does not concern us too much in this book because the existence of sonar has been proved only in the dolphins kept in marine aquaria. However, streams of clicks, of the same sort as those emitted by echolocating dolphins, have been recorded for sperm whales and other toothed whales. There is every reason to believe that sperm whales do use sonar and it is difficult to think how else they can capture squid in the pitch darkness of the depths. There is less evidence for the ability of whalebone whales to use sonar. Recordings have been made of clicks of the type which could be used in sonar but this is a far cry from demonstrating the use of echolocation by any species. Such sounds are equally useful for communication between whales.

The use of the voice for communication between whales has only recently received serious study. The voices of whales have been known as long as their sense of hearing. The Ancient Greeks knew that dolphins sometimes uttered groans and squeals and British whalers of the eighteenth century gave the beluga the name 'sea canary' because they could sometimes hear it trilling like a songbird. Observations in marine aquaria show that the trills are accompanied by a stream of bubbles from the blowhole, and as whales lack vocal chords, the sounds are probably generated by air flowing past folds in the larynx.

The function of the various calls that have been recorded is most likely to keep a group of animals in contact with each other and the subject of communication is discussed in Chapter 6.

The sense of smell can play little part in the life of an animal that spends most of its life underwater with its nostrils shut. Clearly a whale would choke if it allowed water to pass down its nasal passages so there is no way of getting odiferous molecules to the organ of smell. Indeed, toothed whales have no organ of smell and no olfactory bulb, the part of the brain concerned with smelling. Whalebone whales do have a simple organ of smell, an olfactory nerve and a small olfactory bulb. Presumably they can detect smells when they blow, but what use this is to them is not known. Taste is also very rudimentary in whales, although this registers the sensation of chemicals dissolved in water and so might be considered important in a marine animal. However, it is a general rule that a poor sense of taste is found in animals which swallow their food whole, as do whales. The toothed whales seem to have a slight sense of taste but even this appears to be lacking in whalebone whales.

Compared with smell and taste, the sense of touch is well developed. Dolphins kept in marine aquaria are very sensitive to touch. They are fond of being stroked and patted, and will rub their bodies against objects. This shows a general sensitivity to touch on the body. There are also pits on the snout, the remains of hair follicles in the new-born calf, each of which is richly supplied by nerves and may be sensitive to changes in water pressure. There are similar organs of touch around the lips of whalebone whales, which are known to be very sensitive. They have been examined in sei whales, and presumably they will be found in other rorquals.

A sei whale has about eighty short, stiff hairs, 1·5–2·5 centimetres long, disposed about its upper and lower lips. Each one has what appear to be touch-sense cells grouped around the root and it has been suggested that they are used for sensing the flow of water past the body or low frequency vibrations. Sensation of water flow would give the hairs the function of a speedometer and the ability to detect low frequencies might be helpful in navigation as they would be set up by the movements of prey and the swirling of water around rocks and other objects. Other supposed organs of touch are small tubercles, about one millimetre across, which are found inside the lips, around the lining of the mouth and on the tongue. These may also be for sensing food and water movements, but like so much else about the senses of these large and inaccessible animals we have no means of telling.

Sieving Shrimps and Catching Squid

EVER since the story of Jonah being swallowed by 'a great fish' there have been misconceptions as to the size and sort of food eaten by whales. The story of Jonah is an allegory, but among the legends of seagoing peoples there are many stories of whales attacking and devouring men. There is an authentic record of a man being swallowed by a sperm whale after falling overboard. The whale was killed but the man did not even have the luck of Jonah. He had been crushed to death. Nevertheless, there are no proven records of man-eating or even of deliberate man-killing by whales, although when whales were pursued in small boats many men were killed by the quarry lashing out with its flukes or charging the boat. Even the killer whale, the only cetacean to prey on large vertebrates, has never been proved guilty of homicide.

In opposition to the idea of man-eating whales, there is the theory that the whalebone whales are unable to swallow large prey. John Evelyn, the diarist, told of a whale, evidently a right whale, that was stranded in the Thames below London in 1658. He described the throat as being so small that not even the smallest fish could pass through it, but Evelyn had not realized that the throat collapses after death. Nearer the present day, Rudyard Kipling was also unaware of this when he wrote the story of 'How the Whale got his Throat'. The whale in his Just-So story started as a man-eater which swallowed a shipwrecked mariner on his raft. Eventually the mariner was put ashore, like Jonah, but before leaving the whale he blocked its throat with a grating made from his raft. Ever afterwards the whale could eat nothing 'except very, very small fish'. To anyone raised on Kipling's Just-So stories it may come as a surprise that whalebone whales often do feed on fish and sometimes swallow seabirds as large as penguins and cormorants. Nevertheless, whales attract attention because they are huge animals which eat minute food.

Anyone looking over the side of a boat into clear seawater will be lucky to see anything drifting or swimming in it; but pull up a bucketful and take a closer look. There may be some small, almost transparent animals visible to the naked eye and there will certainly be myriads of tiny organisms revealed by a microscope. These are of more than passing interest because they are the key to life in the sea, and they are the means by which the whales, millions of times larger, are sustained. Collectively, these organisms are called plankton, from a Greek word meaning 'that which drifts'.

The basis of this floating life are minute plants, called phytoplankton. Like the familiar plants on land, they make their food by photosynthesis, absorbing sunlight and using its energy to build carbon dioxide and water into carbohydrates. The swarming plants of the phytoplankton grow and breed prolifically. The American expert on seabirds, Robert Cushman Murphy, called these plants the 'pastures of the sea' because the swarms are eaten in colossal numbers by the small animals, the zooplankton. Zooplankton includes crustaceans, jellyfish, sea snails, sea urchin larvae and many others. Some can do no more than float passively. Others have limited powers of movement. But in general they are just swept around by the currents. The planktonic animals, in turn, form the food of the familiar animals: fish, squid, seabirds and the whalebone whales.

The succession of eaters and eaten is known as a food chain and the main food chain of the whalebone whales is possibly the simplest that is in the oceans. It is phytoplankton → zooplankton → whales, although we shall see that one or two extra links are added to the chain when the whales feed on fish or squid.

The food chain of whalebone whales has been studied especially in the Antarctic, first by the scientists of the British Discovery expeditions and later by those of other nations. It might be thought that the cold waters of the Antarctic would have little life, but they are amongst the richest in the world. In the Southern Ocean water rich in nutrient salts containing the nitrogen and phosphorus essential for growth wells up to the surface to feed the phytoplankton, and the greater

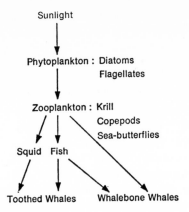

Figure 6 Food chains of whales.

solubility of gases in cold water ensures that there is plenty of carbon dioxide and oxygen for photosynthesis and respiration. The physical fertility of the Antarctic waters allows a wealth of phytoplankton, mainly diatoms, to flourish. These support swarms of planktonic animals which make up the diet of whales which come down to the Antarctic to gorge each summer in the classic three-link food chain.

Chief among the small animals feeding on the masses of Antarctic phytoplankton are crustaceans that resemble but are not very closely related to shrimps and prawns. Their scientific name is *Euphausia*, often anglicized to euphausians, but they are commonly known as krill, a Norwegian name merely meaning 'whalefood'. Krill are found near the surface of the sea because the phytoplankton on which they feed must live at the surface where plenty of sunlight penetrates. There are many species of euphausian in the world's oceans but the most famous is *Euphausia superba*, 60–70 millimetres long, which lives in the ice-covered parts of the Southern Ocean and in the fringing open water. Because of its importance in the diet of Antarctic whales, *Euphausia superba* has received considerable attention from scientists, yet its full life-history is still not known for certain. What is very clear is that it gathers in vast swarms visible to the naked eye as red-brown patches, up to 500 metres long and 200 metres across. These huge concentrations are probably brought together by eddy currents or upwellings and they may persist for several weeks. They are densest in the centre, where there may be about fifteen kilograms of krill per cubic metre of water.

The average density of krill in Antarctic waters is much less than this, but an indication of the vast amounts present can be given by estimates that have been made of the weight of krill eaten by whales. In one day a blue whale eats four meals comprising about four tons, which is about eight million krill, and a fin whale eats just under three tons. There were one million whales visiting Antarctic seas each summer; now there are no more than a third of this number. The original population consumed millions of tons of krill, mainly *Euphausia superba*. With the blue whales, right whales and humpbacks almost wiped out, and other species greatly depleted, there must be a vast uneaten surplus of krill, which, according to some estimates, could amount to something like 150 million tons per year.

What is happening to this presumed surplus? The Southern Ocean is so vast and remote that it is difficult to attempt accurate estimates of the total krill population and so find out whether the amount is increasing. There is a suggestion that other krill eaters, such as the seabirds, penguins and seals, would increase as the whales diminished, but only very recently have we been able to get good estimates of the populations of these animals. We have very little idea of their numbers before whale numbers plummeted but there are some indications that this 'krill surplus' is being put to good use.

Among the whales themselves, there are changes in life-history which suggest that they are reacting to abundant food (p. 89). Observations on whales brought into whaling factories over the last two or three decades have shown an increased pregnancy rate (i.e. an increased percentage of mature females pregnant in any year) among blue, fin and sei whales. Furthermore, among blues and fins the age at which females become sexually mature has decreased because they are growing faster than previously. Similarly female crabeater seals, a very abundant species which feeds almost exclusively on krill despite its name, started to become mature at two-and-a-half years during the 1960s instead of at four years as they did prior to 1955. At South Georgia, the scene of the densest population of whales and the greatest slaughter, the once nearly extinct fur seal has increased from about one hundred individuals in 1936 to 350,000 in 1976. Around South Georgia, fur seals eat krill. Colonies of krill-eating Adélie and chinstrap penguins have enlarged in recent years and there is a possibility that the blue whitefish has invaded the Southern Ocean from Patagonia. Large shoals are attracting the attention of Russian trawlers, yet twenty-five years ago the species had not been recorded in Antarctic waters.

The question naturally arises as to whether we could harvest some of this krill for our own use? It takes ten tons of krill to grow one ton of whale, so it would be more efficient to catch krill and use it for human consumption, than to kill whales. This does indeed seem to be possible as ships from several nations – Russia, Poland, West Germany and Japan among others – are at work in the Southern Ocean catching large quantities of krill. The harvesting is not such a problem as marketing the catch. Krill decomposes rapidly and it has to be quickly processed either into a meal for feeding to farm animals or into a product for human consumption. The Russians and Japanese have marketed krill pastes and krill 'tails' on a small scale, but the exercise will only be worthwhile if krill can be sold in large quantities, cheaply and in a palatable form.

This appears to be a digression from the feeding habits of whalebone whales, but an appreciation of the size of the swarms of planktonic animals in the sea makes it easier to understand the feeding mechanism of these whales. Whalebone whales must have a food that is very abundant. They are huge animals, the largest weighing well over one hundred tons, and, as we have seen, they need several tons of food each day. Therefore their food must be available in enormous quantities. A stickleback can survive by snapping at individual water fleas but a whalebone whale cannot afford to select each tiny item of food and must be able to engulf masses of food with the minimum expenditure of energy.

The fringe of baleen suspended from the palate of whalebone whales is admirably suited to this task, whereas teeth would be virtually useless. The plates act as sieves removing the krill from the water as it flows between them. Similar mechanisms are found in other animals that feed on plankton. The largest sharks, the whale shark and the basking shark, feed on small crustaceans by straining them on projections of the gills called gill rakers. Herring also possess gill rakers and flamingos have rows of plates in their bills for sieving out algae. The krill themselves are filter feeders, trapping minute plants and animals on feathery growths at the base of their legs.

The baleen plates are made from keratin, the same substance as hair and nails. Each plate is made up of hollow fibres enclosed in a horny sheath which gives maximum strength with minimum weight. The plates grow from the roof of the mouth and, like nails, are continuously being worn away and replaced. There are 150–400 plates on each side of the mouth, depending on the species of whale. Each plate is less than 0·5 centimetre thick, but may be up to 4 metres long in right whales. The plates are set about 1–1½ centimetres apart and the fibres on the inside edge separate to make a matted fringe that intermeshes with the fibres of neighbouring plates. This mesh is the strainer which is used for sifting food from the sea.

In a right whale the mouth is an enormous vault supported by the huge arches of the upper jaws. From these hang the baleen plates, 2·48 metres long in Biscayan right whales and 3 metres or more in Greenland right whales. These are protected by 1·5 metres high lips rising from the lower jaws. Right whale baleen is very flexible and, with the mouth shut, the plates fold back towards the throat. When feeding, a right whale opens its mouth and the baleen snaps open like the slats of a Venetian blind. It ploughs through the upper layers of the sea, mouth agape like a gigantic bulldozer collecting everything in its scoop. Water gushes in and is forced out between the baleen plates where the plankton is trapped. At intervals the mouth shuts and the tongue is somehow used to scrape the accumulated food off the network of fringes and push it back into the throat.

In the streamlined head of the rorqual, the baleen plates are shorter and broader at the base than in the deep, bottle-shape of the right whale. In both types the length of the plates

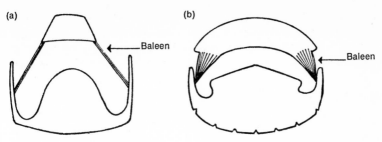

Figure 7 Sections through the head of (a) a right whale and (b) a rorqual, to show the baleen.

shortens towards the tip of the snout so as to leave a gap for the water to enter. Unlike the right whales which open the mouth wide to make full use of the long baleen, the rorquals only part their lips slightly so that the tips of the baleen remain inside the lower lip. This arrangement does not make a very good scoop and the rorquals feed by sucking in water rather than by bulldozing through the sea. The bottom of the mouth can drop to increase the volume of the mouth (compare a picture of a live rorqual and its hollow chin with the flabby jowls of a carcase). Rorquals, then, take a series of massive gulps, sucking in large quantities of water, closing the mouth and squeezing the water out through the baleen with the tongue.

It stands to reason that whalebone whales cannot chew their food; it has to be swallowed whole. The preliminaries to digestion which are carried out by chewing in other animals are carried out in a complex system of stomach compartments. The exact arrangement varies between different species. As in birds, which are also unable to chew, the food is first stored in a bag, equivalent to the bird's crop. The wall of this compartment can expand to receive a meal and then contract progressively to push the food into the next two compartments. These form the stomach proper where digestive enzymes are secreted from glands to break down the food. In some whales the third compartment is barely distinguishable from the second. The fourth compartment receives digestive enzymes from the liver and pancreas.

Some of the older books on whales give the impression that whalebone whales feed almost exclusively on krill and that the *Euphausia* is the only kind of krill. This is because the early work by the Discovery scientists was concentrated in the Southern Ocean where *Euphausia* is by far the main constituent of the zooplankton, and Antarctic whales, particularly those in the rich feeding grounds around South Georgia, feed on little else.

Figure 8 Whale food: krill (*Euphausia*).

Our knowledge of the diet of whales has come from examination of their stomachs as they are cut up at the factory. This is not so easy a task as it might seem because a whale often vomits when wounded by a harpoon and even if killed outright, its digestive processes still continue. Unless the whale is brought to the factory and immediately cut up, only a thick soup of partly digested animals will be found in its stomach. As more whale carcases are examined and observations are made of the habits of living whales, the diets of whales are proving to be more complex than was once thought. It is now known that whalebone whales often feed on much larger prey than planktonic animals and can catch such active animals as herring and squid in sufficient numbers to show that they are not just being swallowed accidentally, as are the penguins and cormorants that have occasionally been found in whale stomachs.

Even around South Georgia, krill is not the only food taken. The right whales which once thronged the bays and fjords of this island had almost disappeared by the time the *Discovery* arrived. Half a dozen specimens were examined early in the century and a few more in the 1920s. The diet was krill. Within the last few years has come evidence that South Georgia right whales may be eating something else. Ornithologists working on the island have noticed that, on occasion, thousands of dove prions, delicate pale grey members of the petrel family, gather in rafts to feed on the surface of the sea. The whalers used to call prions whalebirds because their beaks are fringed with horny lamellae or plates which not only look like baleen but act in the same way. The prions' food is copepods, tiny crustaceans usually of the genus *Calanus*, which the Norwegian whalers call 'brit'.

Sometimes an upwelling or eddy in the sea concentrates the copepods into a dense swarm which attracts the rafts of prions. The ornithologists noticed that right whales sometimes appeared in the vicinity of the prion rafts, maybe three or four together cruising up and down at the surface. Right whales are known to feed on copepods in other areas, off Cape Cod and Japan for instance, and the importance of this observation is to show that the Antarctic population is not so dependent on krill as is sometimes thought.

Indeed, the Antarctic sei whales feed mainly on copepods and the species taken varies with latitude. Starting at latitude 40°S, the sei whales first show a preference for *Calanus tonsus*, then *Calanus simillimius*. Just north of the Antarctic Convergence, they take a small species of krill, *Euphausia vallentini*, and an amphipod crustacean *Parathemisto gaudichaudi*. *Parathemisto* is a carnivorous member of the zooplankton which feeds on smaller animals such as copepods and the larvae of other planktonic animals. Feeding on *Parathemisto*, therefore, represents an extension of the basic whale food chain to: phytoplankton → small zooplankton → *Parathemisto* → sei whale. At the southern of the sei whale's range, along the fringes of the ice pack, its food, and that of the other whalebone whales, is mainly krill, *Euphausia superba*. Even here, diet is not uniform. The blue whale prefers krill with body lengths of 20–30 millimetres, the fin whale takes older animals of 30–40 millimetres length while the minke takes small krill 10–20 millimetres long.

Outside the Antarctic seas, the diets of whales become more varied and it is not easy to give a concise summary of the preferences of each species. The neatest way to summarize the feeding habits of whalebone whales is to say that they are opportunists with preferences. They tend to eat whatever is abundant but each species appears to have a preference for certain food. The sei whale was once thought to specialize in copepods. Its fine, woolly fringes looked eminently suitable for straining small zooplankton when compared with the coarser fringes of other species. This supposition is supported by observations of its diet in the Antarctic but it is turned upside down by examination of sei whale diets elsewhere. In Japan the sei whale has long been known as the 'sardine whale' and, overall, it eats anything suitable, which includes sardines, mackerel, herrings and squid. Around the coasts of Patagonia,

	Krill	Squid	Sardine	Octopus
Blue whale	50	1	1	0
Fin whale	410	2	1	0
Sei whale	367	145	168	2
Humpback	6	0	1	0
Sperm whale	2	1,513	4	19

Table II. Food caught by whales in Japanese waters (adapted from Mizue). The figures show the number of stomachs containing a particular item.

New Zealand and elsewhere, sei whales feed on another swarming crustacean known as lobster krill. This is the planktonic larval stage of bottom-living squat lobsters, *Munida*, which get their name from the way they carry their tails tucked under their bodies. Fin whales have a similarly wide diet. In the North Atlantic the Norwegians used to call them 'herring whales' and they were 'herring hogs' to the British. Capelin, a member of the salmon family which lives in huge shoals in North American seas, and Alaskan pollack attract the attentions of fin whales.

Humpback whales have been recorded as eating krill, lobster krill, squid and fishes. Minkes eat krill, copepods and fish, including bottom-living dogfish; Bryde's whale even tackles small sharks, along with sardines and anchovies. The blue whale is more conservative than the others. It concentrates on krill, either *Euphausia* in the Southern Ocean or *Thysanoessa* and *Meganyctiphanes* in the northern hemisphere.

The whalebone whales can be divided into basic types of feeders: the skimmers and the gulpers. The skimmers include the right whales which plough through the sea with their mouths widely agape so that a current of water passes continually through the baleen. The gulpers – blue, fin, Bryde's, minke and humpback – take intermittent mouthfuls of water by

4. Humpback whale inhaling as its 'blow' disperses. Note the knobs around the blowhole

5. Admission to the Whale Patter's Club. A minke whale surfaces at a small hole in the ice. The seals are crabeaters

6. The Whale Patter's Club treating a killer whale with respect. Note the distinctive white oval behind the eye

dropping the floor of the mouth, then squeezing their intake through the baleen.

Skimming is used by whales which feed on fairly sparse food. Although right whales feed on dense swarms of copepods at times, they can also feed on low concentrations because skimming allows them to strain very large volumes of water. They cruise up and down, picking out dense patches of food where possible, either at the surface with head showing or submerged. The gulpers cannot feed efficiently on sparse prey and concentrate their efforts on swarming creatures. It is the habit of the gulpers to roll on their sides while feeding. No one seems to have thought of an explanation for this.

The sei whale is both a skimmer and a gulper. It skims for copepods in the manner of a right whale and gulps for fish like other rorquals.

So far no mention has been made of the gray whale. It is classed as a skimmer and feeds on both planktonic crustaceans and fishes, but it is also a bottom feeder. The old whalers used to call it the 'mussel-digger' because they used to see it with the snout covered in mud. Its prey is not mussels but mainly several species of amphipod living shallowly buried in the sea bed. The whale rolls on its side and scoops up a mouthful of mud or sand and, as a result, the baleen becomes worn down and the skin is kept clear of barnacles on one side. Of thirty-one gray whales examined, all except three were right-handed in this respect. This behaviour was seen clearly when a young gray whale was kept in a seaquarium at San Diego. It was fed on dead squid which lay on the bottom of the tank. To pick up its meal, the whale rolled over until almost half on its back, opened its mouth slightly and sucked in the squid under the baleen by pulling back the tongue and dropping the floor of the mouth.

Sometimes whales have been seen feeding by swimming vertically up through a plankton swarm or fish shoal, having first swum in circles apparently to concentrate them. Joshua Slocum was seemingly the first to describe this, in one enormous sentence, in his account of sailing around the world.

I have seen, on the other hand, whales swimming in a circle around a school of herrings, and with mighty exertion, 'bunching' them together in a whirlpool set in motion by

3

their flukes, and when the small fry were all whirled nicely together, one or other of the leviathans, lungeing through the centre with open jaws, take in a boat-load or so at a single mouthful.

Slocum did not identify the species involved but this behaviour has since been recorded in humpbacks and gray whales. A refinement of this behaviour is used by humpbacks which have been seen to release a stream of bubbles while swimming in circles. The bubbles race to the surface to make a circular pen in which the whale's prey is trapped. The whale then swims up through the ring and engulfs the food.

An unsolved problem is how whalebone whales find their food. It is known that dolphins have a system of echolocation, described in the previous chapter, and we may find that whalebone whales have a similar system. Streams of ultrasonic clicks have been recorded from blue and minke whales. Their physical characteristics suggest that they could be part of an echolocation system inferior to that of dolphins but good enough to detect swarms of plankton or fish shoals.

The name alone suggests that the other great group of whales, the toothed whales, have entirely different feeding habits. Toothed whales feed on large, active prey that must be hunted, caught and swallowed one by one. Most toothed whales are provided with rows of conical, often sharp, teeth and these seem to be the perfect equipment for catching the slippery fish and squid that make up their diets. Yet some toothed whales have virtually no teeth. In most species of beaked whales there are just one or two teeth in the lower jaw and these only appear in later life, if they appear at all. In a few species the teeth never appear and only in the Tasmanian beaked whale do all the teeth erupt through the gums. Even the sperm whale, which can have formidable teeth in the lower jaw as well as vestigial ones in the upper jaw, may show no signs of teeth until it is sexually mature.

The absence of well-formed teeth in toothed whales suggests that they need not be used to grasp prey and this is further shown by the finding of barnacles on sperm whale teeth indicating a lack of use. It seems that teeth are 'luxuries' and

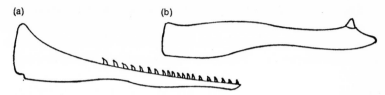

Figure 9 Jaw bones of (a) a sperm whale and (b) a beaked whale (not to scale).

that tough jaws are sufficient to catch fish and squid and toss them back into the throat, unchewed but with the life squeezed out of them. Only the largest prey is dismembered before swallowing. Many seabirds feed in the same way, seizing fish or squid in their horny bills and swallowing them whole or in chunks. In both instances, the food is first stored in a crop and undigested, intact stomach contents are a boon to scientists studying feeding habits. A frequent observation from the old whaling days was of sperm whales regurgitating whole squid during their death throes.

As hunters of squid and fish, toothed whales need to penetrate to greater depths than the whalebone whales. The sperm whale, in particular, often hunts at great depths where it attacks species of squid hardly known to science. The examination of sperm whale stomachs for the indigestible beaks of squid is one of the best sources of information on this group of animals. It has long been known that sperm whales must fight some of the largest squids, such as *Architeuthis*, a monster growing up to 16·76 metres long, of which most is tentacles, and a 14-metre sperm whale harpooned off the Azores was found to have an 18·3 kilogram, 10 metre squid in its stomach. Marks made by the suckers of these squids leave scars 10 centimetres across on the skin of sperm whales and in 1966 a sperm whale was seen fighting on the surface with *Architeuthis dux*, the largest known species of squid. Presumably this fight, witnessed off Newfoundland, had started somewhere in the depths and was continued in the surface when the whale ran out of breath. From the remains found in stomachs it is clear that the whale sometimes wins these battles, but we do not know whether the squid sometimes kills the whale or if the fight ever ends in a draw.

Meals of *Architeuthis dux* and its giant relatives must be exceptional, for stomach contents show that sperm whales usually feed on squid only a metre or so long. They also feed on fish and octopus (see Table II) and most toothed whales have a varied diet. Some beaked whales are known to eat only cuttlefish but others eat cod, herring and salmon, as well as more unlikely animals such as sea-cucumbers and starfish. The beluga or white whale feeds on crabs and shrimps as well as cuttlefish and fish, and sperm whales have been found with the remains of large sharks and seals in their stomachs.

The killer whale deserves a full discussion as it has the widest diet among the cetaceans and has been made famous through stories of its cruel treatment of seals and its fellow whales. This has, however, led to tales of its ferocity being greatly exaggerated. Firstly there used to be a notion that the killer whale uses its tail fin to slice open bodies of other whales. This is pure myth. Another widely credited story is due to a misinterpretation of the findings of the nineteenth-century biologist Eschricht. He published an account of a stranded killer whale. It measured 4·88 metres and he found within it the remains of thirteen porpoises and fourteen seals. This has been taken as twenty-seven whole animals, an impossible figure. What Eschricht really found were fragments of bodies, which must have been accumulated over a fair length of time and were possibly shared with other killers, as they are known to hunt in packs.

The effect of killer whales on other mammals must not be underestimated. The appearance of killers sometimes has the effect of spreading panic amongst seals or sea lions and they make for the shore as fast as possible and even jump into boats. Unlucky seals are snuffed out with a single bite. The whales throw themselves at the seals with such zeal that they run ashore and have to wriggle back into the water. It is reported that gray whales become so terrified that they can only lie helplessly on their backs and are unable to escape, for killer whales even attack whalebone whales, blue whales included. Bands of killer whales have been seen attacking large whales but there is little evidence that they ever kill anything larger than a narwhal or the calf of a whalebone whale; the adults manage to escape with bad cuts. Killer whales do, however, feed on the carcases of large whales and are considered a pest by whalers.

If it is possible to speak of any animal other than Man being cruel, the charge of cruelty can be upheld against killer whales for the way they play with their helpless victims. A group of killers harassed a Californian sea lion for forty-five minutes, pushing and lifting him until he was exhausted and then killing him with a single snap. Sea lions have been seen being thrown far into the air with powerful flicks of a killer's flukes. It is inconceivable that a sea lion could survive such a body-pounding blow, yet the killer may treat the sea lion to several doses of this punishment. These acts echo the domestic cat playing with a mouse in what looks like wanton cruelty and, like a cat, the whales may abandon their victims to sink to the sea bed.

Surprisingly, there is not a single record of man-eating by killer whales. The nearest is Herbert Ponting's story of killer whales trying to tip him into the sea. Ponting was the photographer on Captain Scott's expedition to the South Pole and he had gone to the edge of a large ice floe to photograph a school of killer whales. They disappeared underwater then suddenly the floe started to lurch under him. The killer whales were banging it with their backs, causing the ice to split. As Ponting hopped across the ice fragments to safety, large heads heavily armed with teeth erupted from the surrounding water. Ponting and Captain Scott, who was a witness, both felt that he had been lucky to escape a nasty death as the whales were doing their best to tip him into the water.

From the known habits of killer whales it seems, however, that they were not acting aggressively but out of curiosity. A greater danger comes from the killers' habit of scratching themselves against the hulls of boats. The crew could be thrown out to drown. It is said that the whales catch penguins which have reached the apparent safety of the ice by tipping the floes over and that they use a similar trick to catch sleeping seals and baby walruses. Adult walruses are usually more than a match for a killer whale and they protect their young by carrying them on their backs, but Scammon tells us that a killer whale will come up under the parent, knocking it violently and tossing the youngster into the sea.

In view of the stories attached to the killer whale its diet needs examining in detail. No doubt it varies from place to place, as with other whales, but it is very likely that there has been an undue emphasis placed on the killer whale's predation on mammals. It is at seal colonies and whaling grounds that men will most often see killer whales, if only because that is where men will gather to attack these animals themselves. The killer whales' more mundane fishing activities go unnoticed.

In a study of killer whales caught in Japanese waters it was found that their main food is fish, principally cod and flat-fish, and squid, in roughly equal numbers. The next most frequently found item in their stomachs was dolphins, followed by seals, octopus and finally sharks. Although apparently unsensational, a diet of fish may have more serious conse-quences for man than all the slaughter of whales and seals. In 1952, bands of killer whales invaded the rich fishing grounds off south-west Iceland. They ate the fish and tore up the nets, causing damage valued at tens of thousands of pounds. The Iceland government offered bounties on all killer whales destroyed and later equipped expeditions to hunt them, but with little effect. Finally, the United States Navy was asked to drop depth-charges on the whale packs. They only killed a few of the whales but the harassment was sufficient to drive the rest away to quieter, if poorer, feeding grounds.

6 | Behaviour: Routine and Incredible

THE success of any whale fishery is very largely dependent on knowing where to find whales. The sperm-whalers of the eighteenth and nineteenth centuries discovered by patient searching that there were several regions in both hemispheres where sperm whales might be found in large numbers. The true extent of their distribution was demonstrated by C. H. Townsend who painstakingly investigated and charted the capture of 36,908 sperm whales as recorded in the log books of American whalers between 1761 and 1920. He found that sperm whales are cosmopolitan but are grouped mainly in certain favoured areas, which had been the fishing grounds of the whalers. There was also some degree of movement depending on the season, and the whalers often recorded groups of sperm whales that were obviously on migration. They were swimming in an apparently determined fashion along a compass course, and going too fast to be pursued.

From these observations and the results of the analysis of modern catches and marking experiments a pattern of the movements of sperm whales has emerged. The majority spend most of their lives in tropical or warm seas, probably crossing the equator to get the benefit of the summer in each hemisphere. Only some of the males wander more widely and penetrate the cold waters of the Arctic and Antarctic.

The concentration of sperm whales on the main fishing grounds of the old whalers is due to an abundance of food in these areas. The squid on which they feed are particularly abundant where there is a meeting and mixing of warm and cool water. Hence important sperm-whaling grounds were located along the west coast of South America up to the equator, where the cool Humboldt Current runs northwards, and off the south-west coast of Africa which is influenced by the Benguela Current.

The migrations of whalebone whales are more marked than those of sperm whales. They spend the summer months dispersed over the feeding grounds where there are rich supplies of crustaceans in polar waters, then move to warm water nearer the equator to spend the winter where there is little, if any, food. The reason for the migrations is two-fold. The polar seas are extremely productive and during the summer months

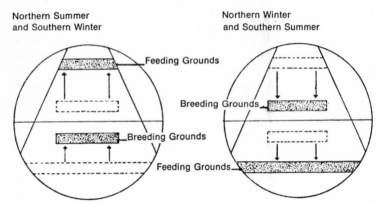

Figure 10 Outline of the migrations of whalebone whales (modified from Mackintosh).

there are large accumulations of the planktonic crustaceans on which whalebone whales feed. The whales gorge themselves during the short summer and then retreat before the sea freezes and cuts off the food supply. They make their way to warmer regions where there are few chances to feed and they have to survive on the reserves of blubber accumulated during the summer. During the winter the whales gather on particular breeding grounds where courtship and birth take place without the distraction of having to feed. As the calves are born with little blubber, the warmer waters of temperate seas may make their early life considerably easier.

These migrations are as definite as those of geese flying to their Arctic nesting grounds or caribou threading their way through the Canadian forests to spend the summer on the tundra beyond. Schools of whales can be seen travelling north or south at certain times of the year and those species that migrate close to the shore, the right whales, the humpback and the gray whale, suffered particularly at the hands of hunters who could harry them in short forays from the shore.

Evidence that these migrations take place is conclusive, but very little is known about the routes taken, even for the coast-hugging species, and, with the exception of the Californian gray whale which breeds in lagoons, virtually nothing is known about the whereabouts of the summer breeding grounds. Now that the numbers of whalebone whales have been so much reduced by hunting the chances of tracing the migration routes and the breeding grounds are slight. It is not impossible that hunting has caused the whales to alter their itineraries and that their breeding grounds are sited well clear of the regular shipping lanes.

The study of migration has been most rewarding where the whales move almost within sight of land. The Californian gray whale leaves its feeding grounds in the Bering Sea some time in October and makes its way down 8,000 kilometres of coast-line to Baja California. In March or April the return journey is made with the newborn calves. On the other side of the Pacific Ocean a few gray whales will be swimming away from the region of Korea and passing up the Gulf of Tartary to the Sea of Okhotsk where they feed in isolation from their Californian cousins in the Bering Sea.

The separation of distinct populations on breeding and feeding grounds has been found in other whalebone whales.

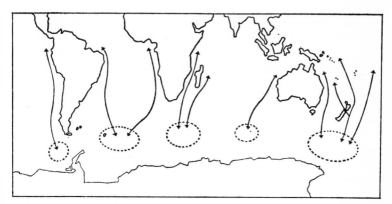

Figure 11 The principal feeding grounds and migration routes of the humpback whale in the southern hemisphere.

The southern populations of humpback whales are divided into five or six groups, as shown by recoveries of whale marks and observations on the movements of the whales. Each group feeds in a fairly restricted zone of the Antarctic (see Figure 11) and migrates north to breeding grounds that are usually in shallow water. Migration is slow and, although individual whales swim at five to six knots, they seem to spend some time wandering about so that the overall movement north or south is very much slower. The speed of the whales is probably geared to fit with the needs of the annual cycle: arriving in the tropics in time to give birth and returning to the Antarctic after the ice has retreated. Nursing cows and their calves are the last to move south and the first to move north so they spend the least time in cold water.

Blue whales and fin whales are known to follow roughly the same pattern of movements as the humpback whales, as summarized in Figure 10, but they spread out more on the feeding grounds and do not appear to gather on restricted breeding grounds. However, it seems that they, too, are divided into distinct populations so that wherever a whale wanders during the summer it returns to the same breeding grounds in winter. There are some exceptions and a few whales marked in one breeding ground have been recovered in another. As the southern winter is at the opposite time of year to the northern winter there is very little chance of whales from northern and southern populations intermingling around the equator but a few hang around on the breeding grounds and may meet, and breed with the other population. Perhaps this is why there are not separate species in north and south hemispheres, except perhaps for right whales which migrate less far.

The study of living animals has turned increasingly to answering questions about the way that they arrange their social life. Individual animals are not identical. They differ in sex, age and in social rank and, within a community, each has its alloted place which depends on its relations with its companions. The organization of the community, in turn, depends on the environment it lives in, its food supply, its predators and so on. The complex interactions between the members of the community are studied by following known individuals over a period of months or years. The most famous of these studies is that made by Jane Goodall on a group of chimpanzees. She knew them so well that she could give them names and they became tame enough for her to follow their daily activities. There are obvious problems in attempting a similar study of the social life of whales but a start has been made by following whales in boats and by SCUBA divers. Individual whales have been identified by nicks in their fins, patches of coloration or other physical oddities and attempts have been made to track them by attaching radio transmitters.

As with any other gregarious animal, the whales are organized in their social life. A gathering of cetaceans at a rich feeding ground may be a chance affair but within the herd there are units which live together, albeit without the constancy of a human family. In contrast to many land mammals, the oceanic cetaceans do not have a territory which they defend against others of their kind; it is difficult to see how they could defend its boundaries. Neither, of course can they have a permanent resting place like a burrow or perch. Nevertheless, there is some evidence that individuals may occupy the same area of sea year after year as if they have a concept of home, and male whales must regard their harem of females as a sort of mobile territory to be defended against other males.

On the whole, the toothed whales are more sociable than the baleen whales. Schools of dolphins and pilot whales may number hundreds, and the largest schools of sperm whales contain over one hundred individuals. Rorquals and right whales, on the other hand, rarely gather in groups of more than half a dozen.

By trailing dolphins in small boats and identifying individuals, evidence is accruing that large schools are composed both of small, fairly stable units and of individuals which join the school for a short time, then leave. It may eventually be proved that the units are extended families, as in a flock of sheep where an old matriarch is followed by her lambs, her grown-up daughters and their lambs. A major problem in studying the social life of whales is the difficulty of determining sex and age. Calves are easy to distinguish but older age groups are virtually impossible. Killer whales make things easier with the tall fins of the mature males and the calves' yellowish colouring on the normally white areas of the skin, but the best known species is the sperm whale.

The usual size of a sperm whale school is around a score of individuals; larger groups are probably formed when several schools combine. Sperm whales are polygamous. The big bulls take charge of harems of females and their offspring and drive away rival males. Violent fights sometimes ensue and bulls suffer from deformed jaws which have been broken in combat and healed crooked. At first sight sperm whale society seems to be patriarchal but the fundamental unit is the matriarchal nursery group of mature cows, their calves and some adolescents. The big bulls contend for access and mating rights in the nurseries but their association is temporary. Bulls come and go but the nursery continues. The adolescents go off to form mixed-sex 'juvenile schools'. Cows return to the nurseries when sexually mature but bulls bide their time in bachelor schools until they are large and powerful enough to contend for access to the nursery. Outside the breeding season, the big bulls lead solitary lives. The system of female dominated nurseries with sexually mature males leading a separate club life until physically mature and capable of fighting their largest peers has counterparts in social land mammals, from deer and elephants to lions and badgers, and monkeys and mice, and is commonly seen among the seals. The human ideal of the permanent two-parent family unit is not shared by the majority of the mammals.

Social behaviour in any animal implies that they must communicate in some way and some form of communication is necessary to bring whales together in schools and to synchronize the behaviour of the members. Whales have long been known to make a variety of rasps, whistles, groans and other noises, apart from the clicks used in sonar, and the obvious assumption is that these are used in communication. The recording of these calls has not been easy but the results have suggested that vocal communication by the whales may be very important.

Sperm whales emit series of clicks and analysis has shown that the clicks coming from a single whale share certain characteristics of pitch and duration and that these characteristics differ in the clicks from another whale. In other words, each whale has an individual voice and, therefore, it is theoretically possible for sperm whales to identify each other by sound. What the whales tell each other is a complete mystery. The white whale earned its name of sea canary from a rich variety of calls which, according to one writer, include 'clicks, whistles, modulated whistles, yelps, trills, blares, rasps, whinnies, squawks, growls, roars, cackles and squalls'. It seems impossible that they do not use this vocabulary for communication. Similarly, the captive killer whale, Namu, has a form of grammar. It can 'abbreviate, punctuate, syllabify, hyphenate; prefix and give numerous endings and inflections'. But there is a huge step to understanding what whales are saying to each other, and talking with them is a pipe dream.

The size of the problem is shown by the story of the songs of the humpback whale. Whalebone whales are normally rather silent animals but at certain times, humpbacks become very noisy. Their calls were first recorded by Roger Payne as they passed Bermuda on their migration down the coast of America. The sounds of a humpback form a series of low pulses and tones that sweep up and down the scale. The series continues for many minutes but they fall into a pattern that is repeated. The whales are singing like birds; they are uttering a set sequence of sounds over and over in the form of a signature tune. These are the 'songs of the whale' made famous on radio and television broadcasts, in conservationist publicity and as a background to folk song.

Since singing humpbacks were recorded off Bermuda they have been recorded in greater detail in the waters around Hawaii. The structure of the songs – the tunes – have been analysed and various characteristics of humpback song made clear. Songs are never heard on the polar feeding grounds. They start as the whales head for warmer waters. All the whales in one population sing the same song which slowly changes over the season, but next year they will start with the tune with which they finish the current season. Apparently only males sing. There is still no explanation as to why they do so. The obvious suggestion is that the songs are 'contact-notes', the ornithologist's name for the twittering calls given by flocks of woodland birds to keep in touch as they forage among the foliage. Divers report that swimming near a singing whale is like standing next to the bass pipes of an organ. The colossal output of sound energy is felt as well as heard and the excellent conduction of sound through water makes it theoretically possible for a whale's calls of 'Here I am' to be heard over huge distances.

The humpback whale's habit of leaping clear of the water and coming down with a resounding smack has been suggested as a form of display or long distance communication. These whales also smack their foreflippers on the surface, making a noise which can be heard for miles. Sperm whales are another species which jumps out of the water – 'breaching' the whalers used to call it – but communication is only one of several functions ascribed to this behaviour. It could be a means of removing parasitic barnacles and whale lice, or the whales may be merely jumping for joy in the way that they indulge in frolics and gambols, splashing and rolling at the surface.

Swimming together in schools and calling to keep in touch is not necessarily evidence of a well-developed social instinct, but there is some indication, unfortunately very limited, that whales take notice of their companions for reasons beyond the call of procreation and that they have social instincts that give them a high rank in the animal kingdom.

It is not uncommon for animals to come to the assistance of their young and in whales the first parental duty is to raise a newborn calf to the surface for its first breath. The parents also react to their offsprings' distress and sperm whales have been known to rescue injured calves by taking them in their mouths. Furthermore, it is not only the mother that reacts to a calf in distress. When a sperm whale calf was wounded by the propeller of the French research ship *Calypso*, a large number of adults were attracted to the scene by its distress calls.

Rescuing behaviour is not confined to assisting calves but is also elicited by injured adults. It is probably a very good indicator of a well-developed social sense, as this behaviour is very rare even among the more intelligent land animals. There are several cases on record of both whalebone whales and toothed whales supporting injured companions at the surface. However, it is often asserted that, while males will come to the assistance of females, the latter will desert their mates.

Another form of co-operation among whales is shown by packs of killer whales which hunt together and are said to surround groups of seals or porpoises and cut off their retreat until they can single out a suitable victim. This leads to the most remarkable whale story of all time: the account of the co-operation between packs of killer whales and the whalers of Twofold Bay, in New South Wales. Friendly dolphins, like Opo of Opononi Beach near Auckland, New Zealand, have allowed people to ride on their backs and play with them, but the killer whales of Twofold Bay actually helped men to catch humpback whales. The killers were said to alert the whalers when a humpback appeared by leaping out of the water and splashing down. The whalers would then launch a boat and chase after the humpback with the assistance of the killers who tried to prevent it from sounding and even attempted to hinder its breathing by leaping on its blowhole. After the whale had been harpooned and despatched, the killer whales were allowed to remove the tongue and lips before the carcase was towed to the shore.

This story is recounted by Professor John Dakin in his book *Whalemen Adventurers* and he is at pains to explain that he was sceptical of the story at first but that he interviewed several of the whalers who had formerly taken part in the co-operative hunts and was sufficiently impressed by their accounts to feel that the story had to be accepted. The intelligence displayed by cetaceans in marine aquaria and their co-operation with their keepers would suggest that it is not beyond the mental ability of killer whales to have behaved in such a way.

What is more surprising is that whales sometimes behave with apparent stupidity and allow themselves to get stranded on beaches, and, when rescued, to swim straight aground again. Some whales can survive stranding; gray whales sometimes voluntarily run aground, later floating free. Right whales have been seen close inshore amongst kelp. Killer whales touch bottom when chasing seals and there is an incredible record of one coming ashore to attack a dog. For the majority of whales stranding means death. With the absence of a surrounding body of water the weight of the body presses on to weak ribs to make breathing difficult and also overheating is likely to occur. The main cause of death is by drowning when the tide returns to cover the blowhole before there is sufficient water to allow the whale to move.

It seems strange that whales should be caught in shallow water and beached. Some stranded whales have, on examination, proved to be diseased or to have parasites in the cavities of the ear or in the central nervous system, which would put out of action any sonar mechanism. It has also been found that gently shelving beaches, where stranding always takes place, are not easily detected by ship-borne sonar. A sick whale, then, might easily overlook gently shoaling water and run aground. Unfortunately for this theory, whales in apparently perfect health sometimes strand. Is it, perhaps, that they are caught off guard, with their minds concentrating on other matters?

For the moment, at least, this must remain one of the many unsolved problems in the study of whales, as must the odd habit of whales coming straight back to the beach after they have been pulled off. In some cases this has happened during a mass stranding and it has been suggested that the whale is returning in response to distress signals being emitted by its comrades still on the beach. Yet whales that have stranded by themselves have sometimes deliberately swum back to the shore after being dragged off. It is all very odd, and it brings up the question of just how intelligent are the whales and dolphins.

The ability of cetaceans to learn, think and talk to each other and to us have become fashionable subjects for speculation and research. Unfortunately speculation has often outstripped solid scientific research. These are extremely difficult topics to work on. One has only to think of the debates concerning intelligence levels among the human species.

While some assert that cetaceans may approach human beings in intelligence, more hard-headed experts suggest a level between dogs and chimpanzees. Leo Harrison Matthews points out that the stories of dolphins rescuing drowning humans cannot be used to demonstrate high intelligence. They should rather drown a member of a species which has persecuted them for centuries. Certainly, rescuing adults or young of their own species need not be a sign of intelligence. Birds, which are not noted for their intelligence, appear quite resourceful in their efforts to lure or drive predators from the nest, but their actions are quite automatic and instinctive.

Even crocodiles, lowly and ancient members of the Reptilia, are caring parents. The danger of interpreting animal behaviour with human motives must be avoided, especially when dealing with such charming animals as whales and dolphins, although there is no reason not to be delighted and amused by human-like actions.

As with other subjects in cetacean study, the bottlenose dolphin provides most of our knowledge on behaviour and mental capacity. Its brain is large and complex but this is not an *a priori* reason for granting it high intelligence. We know little enough about the working of the brain but there is no simple link between structure and function. Nor does a skill at learning tricks indicate great intelligence. Captive and 'tame' wild dolphins do some marvellous things. They are essentially curious and keen to imitate, but so are many animal species which are social and need to seek out their food rather than work their way through it, like a cow. Dolphins do not do anything that other circus animals cannot do, except by virtue of their size, speed and grace, and pet owners will match anecdotes of dolphin intelligence from the behaviour of their cats and dogs, or even their parrots.

There are two final notes of caution when dealing with the intelligence of cetaceans. If it is ever proved beyond the doubt of sceptical scientists that bottlenose or other dolphins are intelligent, it must be remembered that dolphins are not great whales. There is as great a difference between a bottlenose dolphin and a fin whale as between a bushbaby and a chimpanzee, or a gazelle and a bison. A dolphin may need to be as bright as a cat or dog to seek out and catch its prey but a whalebone whale needs no more initiative than a cow. There again, we have to be careful in presuming that cats are more intelligent than cows, despite every appearance that this is so. And if cetaceans are so intelligent, why haven't they made better use of their brains? Man has used his intelligence to control his environment, the cetaceans are still at the mercy of theirs.

7 | Birth and Death

A DISCUSSION of the breeding habits of whales is necessarily brief because we have only the scantiest knowledge about their courtship and parental behaviour. The whalebone whales breed in warmer waters during the time of the year that the whalers are back at home and in areas away from the main shipping routes. However, now that dolphins are being bred in marine aquaria, the processes of their mating and birth have been observed and the courtship and birth of great whales has occasionally been witnessed in the wild.

On the other hand, the physiology of the reproductive cycle, as opposed to breeding behaviour, has received considerable attention from the days of the *Discovery* expeditions onwards. As the carcases were being cut up by the whalers it was possible for zoologists to delve deep into the body cavity, at some risk to life and limb, and recover the reproductive organs. Apart from the likelihood of being drenched in blood from a cut artery or buried under a cascade of entrails, the task is not so simple as a textbook dissection. As the dismembering of the whale proceeds, the organs get pulled out of their proper positions and lost in the general upheaval. Once found, a relatively small organ such as the testis of a blue whale can weigh fifty kilograms and prove difficult to handle.

Examination of the reproductive organs tells the stage of the reproductive cycle the whale had reached when it was killed. For males this means whether it was sexually active or not. The cycle of females is naturally more complex. Examination of the uterus shows whether the whale is pregnant, and at what stage; the mammary glands show whether it was nursing and detailed examination of the ovaries will tell whether the whale was ready to breed again.

One practical drawback to these studies is that they can be carried out only at whaling factories. Most of our knowledge is based on studies of fin and sei whales and humpbacks, where hunting and research has been concentrated in the southern hemisphere during the summer. This means that species which are not hunted have hardly been studied and that nothing can be done outside the whaling season, which is when the whales mate and give birth. Even the breeding grounds are unknown for some species. The Antarctic populations of rorquals appear to move up to about the latitude of Durban and tend to stay in deeper water, but the inshore breeding grounds of gray whales off California, right whales off Patagonia and humpbacks around Hawaii are now so well-known that these whales have become a tourist attraction as well as subjects of scientific study.

We have seen that whalebone whales migrate to warmer water in winter then return to feed in colder water during the summer. The purpose of these migrations, which in gray whales are about 8,000 kilometres each way, is to make use of the seasonal abundance of food during the summer, then to retire to warmer regions which are more favourable for the birth and early life of the young. Newborn whales lack the insulating layer of blubber that their elders possess and would lose too much heat in the cold waters south of the Antarctic Convergence. As it is, not only do mothers with calves migrate to the feeding grounds later than the other females and the males, but they keep to routes that take them through warmer water. Similarly, the calves are led away from the Antarctic before the end of the summer.

The two main events in the breeding of the Antarctic whales take place when the population is in its warm winter quarters. From calculations based on studies of the ovaries taken from fin whales it has been found that fin whales can mate all the year round. However, most of the calves are conceived between April and August. What happens during mating is mostly a mystery. Whalebone whales mate at the surface but it is difficult to see what is happening through the splashing and gambolling of the participants. The actual act of mating takes only a few seconds and may take place with the whales lying horizontally or rearing vertically from the water, belly to belly. Prior to this there is considerable loveplay. Humpbacks have been seen caressing or slapping each other with their flippers or gently swimming past one another with bodies touching. Prolonged loveplay is a feature of the mating of many mammals and in whales it is necessary because scent can play no part in telling the male whether or not the female is in breeding condition. He has to tell by her reaction to his advances.

If the mating is successful, and it is repeated several times, the female whale will carry a single embryo, rarely twins or triplets, down to the Antarctic. During her stay in the breeding grounds she will not have fed and the embryo within her grows at a rate comparable with those of other mammals until she has been feeding for some time. Then it starts to put on weight, at ten times the speed of a human baby. The acceleration may be due to the amount of reserves that the mother can now divert to the developing calf, but a fast growth rate is also essential if the calf is to be ready for birth by the time that the mother returns to warmer water in the autumn.

The actual length of pregnancy has been estimated as eleven and a half months for fin whales, and the other whalebone whales have pregnancies within the range of ten to twelve months. At birth a fin whale calf is 6·1 metres long and a blue whale calf is 7·6 metres long and weighs over two tons. Its growth from a pinhead fertilized egg in eleven months is the fastest rate of growth in the animal kingdom. These colossal babies are as much as one third or more of the mother's length but are only a fraction of her weight. Very few people have witnessed the actual birth of a whalebone whale. Those seen were born head first, although it has always been presumed that they must usually be born, as in dolphins, tail first. The flukes are tucked in and the dorsal fin and flippers are pressed against the body so that they do not catch.

The first action in any cetacean's life is to swim to the surface, perhaps with its mother's help, and take a gulp of air. The first breath is important as it fills the lungs and corrects the buoyancy of the young animal. From then on it can swim well enough to keep up with its mother, staying alongside her dorsal fin or by one of her flippers. A baby whale is less buoyant than an adult because it has very little blubber and this is part of the reason why it is comparatively light in weight for its length. Its dimensions are soon changed as it is fed on a particularly rich milk, three to four times more concentrated than cow's milk, which is said to taste of a mixture of fish, liver, milk of magnesia and oil – a revolting mixture to our taste, but one which obviously makes a very rich diet. The baby blue whale doubles its weight in the first week of life and adds 90 kilograms to its weight every day.

Suckling takes place underwater and the calf is force-fed, taking in a large quantity of milk before it has to surface for breath. The nipple lies in a slit in the mother's abdomen and the calf grabs it between the tongue and the roof of the mouth while milk is pumped in by contractions of muscles around the milk glands.

The mother whale does more than feed her calf. She is jealous for it, warding off other whales and going to its defence. Most of our knowledge of the breeding behaviour of the large whales concerns this last trait. It has been the cause of death or injury to many a whaler when a whale with a calf has turned on her pursuers. In humpbacks, the mother and calf are often accompanied by an escort. The identity of the third whale is not known but it may be an elder but immature sister, as happens in elephant society, or an adult who has no calf of her own. One escort was seen beating off attacks by killer whales, charging them and beating them with her huge flippers.

Charles Scammon, who wrote a very complete account of the gray whale and the methods of hunting it, gives many details of the behaviour of gray whales with calves. This species gives birth to its young in the shallow lagoons that fringe the coasts of California. In the middle of the nineteenth century whalers arrived each year to hunt them. They soon learnt that it was dangerous to harpoon a gray whale calf from an open boat. The enraged mother would attack the boat, butting it with her head or slapping it with her flukes. Despite this danger the whalers preferred to hunt cows with calves because the cow had to keep to the slow pace of her offspring. They also traded on the female's maternal instincts by harpooning the calf from the shore, towing it in and then harpooning the cow as she followed, helplessly, behind it.

Nowadays nursing cows and their calves of all whales are protected, although mistakes are made when the calf wanders from its mother's side. There is every likelihood that the pair of them will survive the period of nursing. In fin whales this lasts for six or seven months and the calf is weaned on its first visit to the Antarctic. This timing is no coincidence as weaning takes place among the rich feeding grounds of the Southern Ocean. Learning to feed itself is a difficult stage in the life of any animal and it is an advantage for the learning period to come during a time of plenty.

By the time they are weaned the baby whales have approximately doubled in length and the weight of a blue whale has shot up from two to twenty-three tons. Growth now slows down and at physical maturity, somewhere between thirteen and fifteen years, it almost ceases. By then blue whales are about 25 metres long and fin whales about 3 metres shorter, with females being a metre or so longer than males in both species.

The whalebone whales considered so far breed once every two years and the major events in the cycle fit the species' pattern of migration to and from the cold feeding grounds. Mating and birth take place in warm water where the adults subsist on their thick layers of blubber, and weaning takes place in cold water where there is an abundance of food. In the toothed whales there is no regular north-south migration and cow sperm whales do not enter cold water. Their breeding cycle is accordingly not fitted in a biennial pattern. The same is also found in one whalebone whale, Bryde's whale, which is confined to warm water all the year round. It mates and gives birth at any season.

Whalebone whales are often said to be promiscuous as the female does not appear to associate with one particular male and sometimes several males are seen consorting with one female. This does not necessarily mean that mating is random. By analogy with other mammals, there may be a hierarchy of dominance among the males which ensures that seniors are the most likely to fertilize the females. Sperm whales and some other toothed whales have a more clearly definite social system (p. 76). Male sperm whales fight amongst each other during the mating season and the victors apparently secure harems of females. The bachelors live in separate herds, some of which travel into polar regions. Male beaked whales carry

one or two pairs of long teeth on the lower jaw. They sometimes show as boar-like tusks when the mouth is shut and, from
the scarring on the bodies of mature bulls it seems that they
are used in fighting.

Mating of sperm whales takes place in the spring and the
pregnancy lasts sixteen months, as it does in killer whales – a
considerably longer period than in whalebone whales. There
are a few records of newborn sperm whales. A Russian ship
found a calf still attached to the umbilical cord. Its tail flukes
were rolled up and its mother and two other adults were
helping to support it. When the ship approached, the mother
pushed the calf to her protected flank. Lactation is also
prolonged in sperm whales and lasts for about a year. Clearly
the breeding of sperm whales does not conform to changing
seasons and the length of the cycle means that they can breed
once in every three years.

Thereafter, however, the young sperm whales reach
maturity at about the same age as whalebone whales, but there
is one difference. Male sperm whales mature at a length of 15
metres but the females mature at 12 metres. The larger size of
the males is maintained throughout life and is probably linked
with their habit of forming harems for mating. Similar size
difference between the sexes are found in those species of seals
in which the male holds a harem. The males of fur seals and
elephant seals are far larger than the females, whereas there is
little size difference between sexes in Weddell seals, common
seals and others, where there is a looser social structure without
so much competition between the males.

After considering the start of a whale's life it is sensible to
examine the other end of its lifespan. It used to be thought that
whales were very long lived, merely because they were very
large. There is no basis for a correlation between size and
lifespan in animals and it turns out that the life of a whale is
not particularly long. A few fin whales have been found with
earplugs that bear eighty laminae and may be around eighty
years old but the average lifespan is more in the order of
twenty-five to thirty years.

Before man discovered the means of slaughtering the great
whales there must have been relatively stable populations of all

species in which the birth rate equalled the death rate. We have seen that whales breed slowly, one calf every two or three years, so the death rate must have been correspondingly low. As with most animals that have been studied, it is the young of the whales that are particularly vulnerable. They may be stillborn or born with serious deformities that condemn them from the start, and they may not survive the period of learning to feed themselves. Furthermore, at this age they are more vulnerable to predation, by killer whales and sharks, and to disease and parasites.

Once fully grown, whales face few hazards, although mature males may receive fatal injuries when fighting. They will not suffer from severe climatic conditions except in the odd situation of being trapped by a frozen sea and prevented from blowing. This is an occurrence that is probably as rare as a mass stranding, but there is one record showing that it is a distinct possibility. In 1957 a British exploring party was travelling down the frozen Crown Prince Gustav Channel, off the mainland of the Antarctic Peninsula. In one place they noticed a series of large pools in the ice through which a number of whales were blowing. There were several minke whales, one killer whale and one beaked whale. The explorers were able to stand at the edge of a pool and touch the whales as they came up. Thus the small and exclusive 'Pat-the-whale' Club was founded. A few weeks later the holes had shrunk to a few yards' diameter and the fate of the whales seemed to be sealed. The explanation for this discovery is that the sea must have frozen across the head of the channel before the whales had a chance to move clear and they were only able to stave off drowning as long as they could keep the vital breathing holes clear.

Stranding (p. 79) is a more common cause of death, but stranding and being trapped by ice must count as fatal accidents that have little significant effect on the adult population. So, it would seem, is the role of predation which is limited to sporadic attacks by killer whales. There is one strange antagonist of whales, the swordfish. Blue whales have been found with the swords of swordfish buried deep in their bodies. The function of the sword is thought to be to kill fish for food, but there are numerous records of swordfish ramming boats either by accident or deliberately. Attacks on whales must be for the same reasons, whatever they might be! Another odd attack comes from a tiny, 45-centimetre shark. Known only by the scientific name of *Isistius brasiliensis*, until nicknamed the cookie-cutter shark by Ken Norris, this fish has been found to be the cause of circular scars and wounds carried by many cetaceans. It grips the skin of the cetacean, or a large fish, with a sucker-like mouth and slices out a divot of flesh with its sharp teeth.

Ice traps, berserk swordfish and nibbling sharks make interesting tales but they do not answer the question of what is the main cause of death among adult whales. Food supply is the important factor that limits the size of many animal populations and this may be the ultimate check on the numbers of whales. If new whales are continually being added to the population, some must go short of food if the supply is not to become exhausted. Once one becomes undernourished it has to draw on its reserves and it will become weaker and less able to resist any further setback. Parasitic infection, injuries and diseases (of which cirrhosis of the liver, tuberculosis and pneumonia have been recorded) will then hasten the end.

The very old and very young whales are those that are particularly at risk from disease and starvation and it is deaths in these two categories that probably balance the population, if our knowledge of other animal populations is anything to go on. It is usual for animals to produce more young than are necessary for the maintenance of the species. The surplus die early and can be considered as a potential reserve that can perhaps survive and grow up if the numbers of adults drop.

With the populations of some species of whales dropping to danger level through overhunting it is to be hoped that there is some means by which the maximum number of offspring can be brought to maturity and so bring about a rapid increase in numbers. The Antarctic whale stocks were reduced to one third of their original numbers and one fifth of their total weight (the whalers preferred to kill the largest whales). Some of the food which would have been eaten by the slaughtered whales appears to have been used by the survivors to speed their breeding rate.

Observations on whales brought into whaling factories over

the last two or three decades have shown an increased pregnancy rate (i.e. an increased percentage of mature females pregnant in any year) among blue, fin and sei whales. Furthermore, among blues and fins the age at which females become sexually mature has decreased because they are growing faster than previously. The age of sexual maturity in Antarctic fin whales has dropped from eleven and a half years in 1957 to six years in 1968.

The whales do, therefore, seem to be recouping their losses, but there are doubts as to whether they will ever regain their former abundance, as in the days when Ross's ship had almost to nudge right whales out of the way. Right whales are appearing again in Antarctic waters but their recovery is painfully slow and some right whale populations show no signs of recouping after decades of protection. The gray whale is often cited as a success for conservation. From the early part of the twentieth century when it looked as if the eastern Pacific population would follow the western Pacific population into extinction, its numbers rose rapidly and levelled out at 11,000. Yet it is substantially lower than the original population of 15,000. Other species will probably fare equally because, in their absence, their food supply has been usurped by other animals; other whale species, or seals, seabirds and fish (p. 58). The few right whales on the Aleutian feeding grounds, for instance, have to compete for copepods with fin whales.

PART II | Whaling

'What do ye do when ye see a whale, men?'
'Sing out for him!' ...
'And what do ye next, men?'
'Lower away, and after him!'
'And what tune is it ye pull to, men?'
'A dead whale or a stove boat!'

'For God's sake, be economical with your lamps and candles! not a gallon you burn, but at least one drop of man's blood was spilled for it.'

HERMAN MELVILLE, Moby Dick

8 | The Foundations of Whaling

THE story of whaling starts before the beginning of history. The kind of whales hunted and the methods of hunting can only be guessed at, but as whaling developed it came to play an increasingly important part in the lives of maritime people. The whaling interests of different countries often clashed so that whalers needed the protection of arms, and they were not immune to outside events. The introduction of petroleum oil for lighting purposes, for example, hastened the eclipse of the sperm whale fishery, not long after the New England fleet had been almost completely destroyed in the American Civil War.

Although the production of whale-oil and whalebone were vital to the economy of these maritime nations, whaling rarely, if ever, appears in their histories. In 1812 there was a war between Britain and America, yet – in British histories, at least – the destruction of the American whaling fleets goes unrecorded. Perhaps this is because whaling appears to the historian as no more than another industry to provide the wealth and material whereby a nation can indulge in the more varied, dramatic and interesting spheres of domestic and foreign politics.

From Melville's quotations at the head of the chapter it would appear that whaling has a drama of its own but the old whalers have left very scanty material on which to bring to life the day-to-day running of their profession. We know virtually nothing of how the Basque whalers operated in the sixteenth century and the situation improves only slightly over the years until William Scoresby, Junior, published his *Account of the Arctic Regions* in 1820. This contains the first full history and description of the whaling industry. Then, in 1874, Charles Scammon published an account of the American whale fishery. These two works contain factual descriptions of the methods of catching and processing whales in different parts of the world and they also give a very clear picture of life in whale-ships, especially vivid in Scoresby's account of the various ways in which danger to life and limb can befall the crew.

The latter half of the eighteenth century and the first half of the nineteenth saw the heyday of the old-fashioned sperm-whaling in which rowing boats and hand harpoons were used for grappling with whales. This is the only phase of whaling that has become familiar through popular writing. It was immortalized by Herman Melville's *Moby Dick* which, although a work of fiction, is largely accurate in its background because Melville himself had sailed in a whale-ship. Nearly fifty years later, in 1900, another masterpiece appeared, Frank Bullen's *The Cruise of the Cachalot*. This is a supposedly true account of a voyage in the whale-ship *Cachalot* that sailed around the world hunting over the same whale-fishing grounds as Melville's ill-fated *Pequod*.

There are other accounts of such voyages, which lasted for three or four years and took their crews around the world, but the style is all too often that of the terse entries in a ship's log with little attempt at description. One of the most unusual narratives is that by Eliza Williams, wife of the captain of the New Bedford ship *Florida*. Whaling captains quite often took their wives to sea and Mrs Williams gave birth to two children during her first two-year voyage. In the same book, one of her sons continues the family's saga with a graphic account of the disaster that befell the American whaling fleet in 1871 and of a Pacific cruise he undertook when a boy.

The last story of old time sperm-whaling is Robert Cushman Murphy's *Logbook for Grace*. This is the charming account by one of America's foremost ornithologists of a voyage in the brig *Daisy*, one of the last of the sailing ships to be employed as a whaler. *Logbook for Grace* forms a link with the present, as the *Daisy* called in at South Georgia where the modern Antarctic whaling industry was being pioneered by C. A. Larsen. From this time onwards the whaling industry is swept up by the modern development of documentation. Each year sees published statistics of whales caught, their products and their value. Scientific studies on the habits of whales pour out, while popular articles and books appear, describing whaling adventures or condemning the rapacity of an industry that is killing off the whales faster than they can breed. There is, however, no modern equivalent of Melville or Bullen, except in *To catch a whale*, Terence Wise's description of lower-deck life on a factory ship and F. D. Ommaney perhaps gives us the equivalent of *Logbook for Grace* in his *South Latitude*.

The whaling industry has sprung up independently in many parts of the world at many different times and this makes an account of its development anything but straightforward. However, it becomes clear from both historical and narrative accounts that wherever whaling has been carried out as an organized industry, its progress has followed a regular, although very general, pattern. At first, catching whales is comparatively easy because of their abundance. Hunters flock after them and because the sale of whale products becomes an important part of the economy, there is no difficulty in finding sponsors for whaling expeditions. Handsome profits can be made but gradually the whale populations are hunted out and the whalers are forced farther afield in search of new stocks. This trend continues until so few whales are left that the industry becomes unprofitable and collapses, perhaps leaving a remnant to eke a living out of the remaining stocks. Occasionally there is a slight recovery of the industry as the whale population revives.

There are two main variations on this pattern. The industry may never expand; in fact it may never really become an industry as in the case of whaling by coastal people such as the Faeroese and Eskimos. They catch whales for the immediate use of the community in much the same way as the Eskimos hunt seals and game for food, clothing and other domestic purposes. In such cases the number of whales killed does not seriously affect the stocks while whaling continues according to the traditional pattern.

Advanced whaling industries may close down before the whale stocks are exhausted through political or economical difficulties. The New England sperm-whaling, for instance, received severe blows from both causes. Many whaling vessels were destroyed during the Civil War, then mineral oil was discovered in 1859 and whale-oil was pushed out of the market for fuel and lubricating oil. Nevertheless, in line with the general pattern, sperm-whalers continued to sail from New England ports until 1925 and transplanted offshoots of the industry still linger in the Azores, Madeira and Santa Lucia.

Another pattern that emerges from the history of whaling is seen in the techniques used. This is not surprising when one considers that, except for primitive peoples who exploited whales mainly for food, whales have been caught principally for the oil in their blubber. Thus whaling always involves three basic processes: (1) capturing and killing, (2) stripping the blubber and (3) extracting oil from the blubber. The methods used in each process have developed along similar lines where-ever whaling has flourished. Even the modern whaling of the twentieth century follows the same plan. Its output and efficiency were changed by the addition of machinery in the same way that the English cotton industry, for instance, was changed by the Industrial Revolution.

Until harpoons with explosive heads were invented, the capturing and killing of a whale were separate operations. The former involved the use of a harpoon, a barbed spear that caught fast in the whale's flesh. A line from the harpoon to the whalers' boat, or to floats, impeded the whale's movements so that it tired sufficiently for the whalers to close with it and attack with long, razor-sharp lances. Once dead, the whale was towed to the shore or the whalers' ship, where it was stripped of its blubber and other valuable parts such as whalebone, the teeth in the case of sperm whales and, latterly, meat and endo-crine organs. This mammoth dissection, known to the American whalers as cutting-in, was a skilled as well as an arduous and often dangerous job. The large slabs of blubber were then cut into small pieces and 'tried-out', that is cooked in large cauldrons to express the oil from the tissue of the blubber.

This, then, is the outline of the course and techniques of the whaling industry. The origins of each are, however, lost because man first started to hunt whales in prehistoric times. There is no doubt that the first whales to be exploited were those that were unfortunate enough to be stranded. The discovery of a school of dolphins or a single rorqual cast up on the beach must have represented a major windfall to primitive

7. A sperm whale in its death throes. The scene shows how the whalers had to deal with the stricken animal at dangerously close range. These crews are lucky to have their ship nearby. The whale making a fountain on the horizon suggests that the artist was not a whaler. (From *The Naturalist's Library* conducted by Sir William Jardine, Bart.)

8. Loading the harpoon gun. Note the wire loop through the shaft and the cords holding the flukes in place. The grenade has not been attached. When the harpoon is in place it is secured by cord to the two lugs on the top of the muzzle

9. Secured by a chain around the tail stock, a whale is towed alongside a catcher

10. A fin whale is cast free with a marker flag and radio beacon. A killer whale surfaces behind it; the birds are storm petrels and an albatross

people who, judging by the habits of some of the aboriginal hunting tribes of today, probably paid little attention to storing food but never lost the opportunity of gorging themselves until sated.

The earliest evidence we have of men deliberately seeking out and killing whales lies in a few drawings scratched on rock faces in Norway. One, estimated to be four thousand years old, was found on the island of Rødday in northern Norway. It depicts a man in a boat, a seal and two porpoises. There is also an elk which does not fit in with the rest of the picture – but a confusion of animals, often painted at different times, is found in the much older cave-paintings at Lascaux. Another picture, at Meling, shows a whale surrounded by boats filled with men, one of which appears to have been upset by the whale's tail, a scene often shown in illustrations of whaling.

These pictures may be idle doodles scratched for fun, as in the case of some modern rock paintings in Africa and Australia, or part of a ritual of sympathetic magic, in which the painting or scratching of an image is supposed to assist in hunting the real animal, but it seems reasonable to suppose that the early Norwegians actively hunted the cetaceans they drew.

Unfortunately, none of these rock carvings show the manner in which these whales were secured but from our knowledge of whaling in historic times three ways seem likely: poisoning, harpooning and driving. The hunters of the north-west Pacific, living in the Aleutian and Kurile Islands, Kamchatka and Hokkaido, pursued large whales in one-man kayaks, as in the Rødday picture. The whales, usually humpbacks, were attacked with spears tipped with a poison extract from the roots of aconite, and were left to die. Several days later the corpse would be washed up on the shore and the owners identified by the marks on the spear. The whale was then divided between the people who killed it and those who found it.

Primitive harpooning of whales was carried out by Indians and Eskimos on both coasts of North America at least until the nineteenth century. Singly, or in groups, the hunters pursued the whales, thrusting harpoons into their backs. Attached to the harpoons were floats of sealskin or wood which resisted the whale's progress as it sounded, tiring it and revealing its

4

position to the waiting hunters. As soon as the hunters could get near, the whale was speared again and again until it was dead.

Scammon records that the Indians of the north-east Pacific hunted gray whales in fleets of canoes, each carrying a crew of eight. When a whale was killed it was towed back to the village and divided up to provide a feast for the whole community, with the surplus oil being sold to tribes from the interior. In the same way as the Indians of the Great Plains and northern forests utilized every part of bison and caribou carcasses, so the coastal Indians and Eskimos had many uses for their whales. The whalebone was used for sledge runners and its fibres were separated to make fishing tackle and nets. Ribs were used for picks and mauls, and Eskimos relish squares of blubber and skin cut from newly killed whales. Known as *mattak*, the skin has a nutty flavour and is particularly rich in vitamins.

Perhaps the most hazardous method of whaling ever practised was the almost suicidal technique of the Florida Indians. Father José de Acosta recorded in 1880 that the whale was chased by canoe until one man could leap onto its back and thrust plugs into its blowholes. If the operation was successful the whale suffocated.

Around the coasts of northern Europe there has long been practised another method of catching whales, the origin of which is lost in pre-history. It probably developed later than the spearing and harpooning of whales just described because, to be successful, it requires the co-operation of a community with elaborate conventions and signalling systems. This is the deliberate driving of a school of whales onto the shore where they can be slaughtered. The species captured is the pilot whale which lives in schools of hundreds and sometimes thousands.

The whole school easily becomes stranded because of a strong herd instinct which leads to the school swimming into shallow water and onto the shore if one or more of their number becomes stranded – perhaps in response to distress signals. The technique is for the hunters to form a semi-circle of boats behind the school and gently guide it towards a convenient beach. When the school is nearly aground one whale is lanced. Panicking, it races shorewards and the rest follow blindly rather than turning and breaking through the cordon of boats.

In the Faeroe Islands where it is known as *grindadrap* – the killing of the *grind* or school – records of pilot-whaling date back to 1584. It also used to take place in the Hebridean, Orkney and Shetland Islands where it was known as *caaing*. As all these island groups were peopled by Norse settlers it seems reasonable to suppose that the custom originated along the coast of Norway where narrow, steep-walled fjords would have eased the task of shepherding the school of whales. The importance of pilot-whaling to the communities of these rather barren islands is shown by the proportion of the Faeroese law books which is taken up with legislature concerning the *grindadrap* and the zeal which the Faeroese show towards the exercise even today, although it is now more of a ritual than a vital economic activity. The most graphic description of Faeroese pilot-whaling is to be found in Kenneth Williamson's *The Atlantic Islands*.

The school of pilot whales is sighted from the shore or from a boat. If the latter, a makeshift flag is waved to alert other boats and people on the shore. Immediately the alarm – the *Grindabod* – is raised and every available person rushes, by car, cart or foot, to the harbour. School children are released for the day, and the only people not welcomed are pregnant women because both in Faeroe and Shetland it was thought that their presence on the beach prevented the whales from landing. Meanwhile the message is passed to other parts of the countryside, originally by a network of messengers and beacons, but now by telephone messages that have priority over all other calls.

The whale school becomes the rallying point for the boats which are placed under the leadership of a captain, whose job is to direct the coaxing of the whales into a harbour. The chosen harbour must have a gently shelving shore of mud or sand on which the whales will be easily stranded. It is selected after a consideration of various factors. For instance, pilot whales prefer to move into the wind so the nearest harbour may not be chosen if it is downwind of the school. It may even be necessary to corral the whales in a cove until conditions become more favourable.

The boatmen take care not to frighten the whales but gently

chivvy them along by dropping into the sea white-painted stones to which lines are attached. As the school nears the beach the captain gives the word and one whale is lanced in the tail so that it springs towards the beach. Its companions follow and the slaughter starts as men thrust at the whales from the boats with lances and knives, or jump overboard to tangle with them at close quarters. At the same time other men wade out from the shore to assist, stabbing at the threshing bodies or planting hooks into them so that they can be dragged ashore by the waiting crowd, while children run underfoot slicing at the bodies.

When the carnage is over it is the turn of the officials, the *metaringarmenn*, who divide the catch using traditional Norse tallies. The distribution of the meat and blubber follows strict rules as laid down by law, although these have been altered to fit modern conditions. The largest whale is given to the boat that first sighted the school, a portion is sold to reimburse men whose gear has been damaged, another portion is used to pay the *metaringarmenn* and other officials, some meat is put aside for the feast that follows and the rest is divided amongst the community. Some fresh meat is boiled but most is dried or salted for winter use. The heart, liver, lips and kidneys are fried and little is discarded except the head and flippers.

In Shetland, the practices were rather different. Except in times of famine only the blubber was used, being sold to merchants, often in exchange for spirits. Perhaps this is why pilot-whaling was less important to the Shetlanders. They also received less of the proceeds, two thirds of the catch going to the Admiral of the County and the landowners where the whales came ashore. The last Shetland *caa* was held in 1903, and pilot whales are now rarely seen off Shetland, but a similar practice survived until recently on the other side of the world where Solomon Islanders drove schools of porpoises ashore. The porpoises were kept on the move by one man in each boat clashing stones together underwater and when they reached the beach they were dragged ashore by the hundreds of islanders that gathered there. The meat was eaten and the teeth were used as currency for buying wives. A necklace of one thousand teeth was the value of a bride.

The killing of schools of whales by Faeroese and Solomon

islanders was more than a slaughterhouse operation providing food and products for trade. There is the thrill of the hunt, felt both in primitive and in civilized communities, culminating in an outburst of blood lust. In Faeroe there are wild celebrations following the division of the catch, and foreigners are sometimes warned to stay indoors. J. G. Millais conveys the universal excitement through an anecdote in which a Shetland preacher noticed that members of his flock were furtively stealing away as word of the arrival of whales spread. He hurriedly wound up his sermon with the words 'Let us all have a fair start – just a fair start' and joined the exodus from his church.

Pilot-whaling was also carried out in Trinity Bay, Newfoundland, where the whales were driven into narrow fjords and imprisoned behind a net. The capture lacked the traditions and excitement of the Faeroes or the Solomon Islands and the carcases were used for a more prosaic purpose: as food for ranch-bred mink.

In Newfoundland 3,000 to 4,000 whales were caught each year and at one time the Faeroese averaged about four hundred a year but whale stranding has also been practised elsewhere on a casual basis. In 1959, a whalebone whale was driven ashore in eastern India by the crews of two fishing boats and dragged up the beach by one hundred and fifty men. The blubber fetched little money but an enclosure was built around the whale and some twenty thousand people paid 2,000 rupees (£150) to see it. During the four days that the whale was on exhibition it was perfumed with agarbathis, frankincense and mothballs.

If the two oldest methods of capturing whales are to drive them ashore or to harpoon them, it seems that the latter is the more practicable. It requires fewer men and less time than the shepherding of a school or an individual whale and it can be done in deep water, well away from land. It is the harpooning and spearing of whales that was developed by the medieval Basques into the organized industry that became the foundation of all later industries, including the worldwide sperm-whaling of the eighteenth and nineteenth centuries and the factory whaling of the present day.

The Basques are generally regarded as the Fathers of

Whaling because they were to teach the secrets of their trade to the English, the Dutch and other nationalities. There is evidence, however, that the Basques originally learned whaling techniques from Norwegians, who, as Normans, settled around the Bay of Biscay.

The first written record of Norwegian whaling appears in an account of a sea journey around Norway to the White Sea given by a Norwegian, Ottar or Ohthere, to King Alfred of Wessex in about the year 890. Ohthere met whalers, but Alfred does not record what whales were hunted or how they were caught except that Ohthere and five companions had killed sixty in two days. The whales were between forty-eight and fifty ells long and could have been whalebone whales, if the Norwegian ell is taken as being approximately one English foot. The two likely species are the Biscayan right whale, which was later hunted by the Basques, and the gray whale. The latter is now extinct in the Atlantic, but its skeleton has been found in the Zuider Zee and there is good evidence that it was once hunted in Icelandic waters and still occurred along the coasts of eastern America in the eighteenth century.

Early Norwegian whalers have also been credited with inventing a giant crossbow or *balista* for use as a harpoon gun, but this may be due to confusion with the use of a crossbow that survived in some Norwegian fjords until recently. When a whale was found in a suitably narrow fjord, its escape was cut off by a line of nets and rusty, dirty crossbow bolts were fired into its back. In due course it died of septicaemia and was hauled out onto a beach.

However, the Norwegians fade out from the mainstream of whaling history until the second half of the nineteenth century when Svend Føyn's invention of the first really practical harpoon gun revolutionized whaling and paved the way for the mechanized whaling of the twentieth century. This was first dominated by the Norwegians, and more recently by the Japanese and Russians. The medieval Japanese had already developed whaling techniques, perhaps borrowing ideas from the Portuguese, producing what must be the oldest heavy industry with production-line methods. In due course they learnt the newer methods that were being developed by western countries, and now they are one of the leading whaling nations.

9 | The Development of an Industry

THE seaside towns of Biarritz, St Jean-de-Luz and St Sebastian are seaside towns made famous as spas or watering places in the early years of this century. Yet these towns, together with others around the south-east corner of the Bay of Biscay, were the home of the first organized whaling industry. Previously, whales had been caught mainly for the immediate benefit of the local community, but here in the Basque provinces of Spain and France, whale products became important items of trade.

The Basques probably started to hunt whales in the tenth century and by the twelfth century their industry was firmly established. It remained so for at least four hundred years. The important part that whaling played in the life of the Basque ports is shown by the number that have whales on their coats-of-arms and by the importance which kings attached to them. At Guetaria the first whale of the season was given to the king, presumably in the form of the cash it realized rather than as an actual carcase, and at Zaruaz the king received a long slice of meat from the back of each whale caught.

At this time the western part of France was in English hands and the English kings taxed all whales brought into Biarritz. In fact, the kings of England were awarded the title of Honorary Harpooner and in 1324 the statute *De Praerogativa Regis* declared whales to be royal fish and therefore the property of the Crown. This royal prerogative fell into disuse many years ago, but it was only in 1970 that an attempt was made to abolish it as an inconvenient relic of the past. It was pointed out that several tons of whale rotting on a holiday beach is a public nuisance, if not a health hazard, and it is inconvenient to have to seek royal assent to its removal. This attempt was eventually frustrated on the grounds that the machinery of reporting carcases enabled the British Museum (Natural

History) to obtain many valuable specimens of whales which would otherwise be lost.

The whales hunted by the Basques were mainly Biscayan right whales, then abounding in large herds whose migration routes led them close inshore. Right whales are so called because they are the right whales to hunt from small boats. They travel slowly and even when hurrying cannot outpace small rowing or sailing boats. Equally important, they do not sink when killed so that it is possible for the small boats to tow carcases back to the shore.

The most valuable products of the right whales were the blubber, which was rendered into oil for lighting purposes, and the whalebone or baleen. Whalebone had a variety of uses which were based on two important properties. It is stiff yet elastic and when immersed in hot water it becomes pliable and can be moulded. This made it an excellent material for corsets, fishing rods, whips, sweeps' brushes, the seats of chairs, springs in machinery and so on. In the nineteenth century when ostrich plumes were high fashion, cheap and barely distinguishable substitutes were made from whalebone. In the seventeenth century whalebone was worth as much as £2,250 per ton and the whalebone from one whale made a whaling cruise profitable, but it has since been superseded by spring steel and plastics. Nowadays, when the maximum profit is squeezed out of each whale, the whalebone is the only part to be discarded, although a little is still used for making brooms and riding crops.

There is no contemporary description of how the Basques caught their whales but we can get a good idea by deduction from what little information exists. Whaling was probably a joint enterprise carried out by the community on the Faeroese pattern, as shown by the remains of look-out towers from which a watch was kept for whales and by the way the catch was divided. In Lequeitio, for instance, the whalebone from each whale was divided into three parts: one part to cover costs for repairing the church and two parts for repairing the harbour.

The town seal of Biarritz, dated 1351, shows a small boat approaching a whale. Three of the crew are rowing or paddling, one is working a steering oar and the fifth is standing in the bows with a harpoon at the ready. So even in this stylized portrayal we see an arrangement similar to that used by the American sperm-whalers and British right-whalers of the eighteenth and nineteenth centuries. This is only to be expected as the English and other European whalers were taught their skills by Basques who sailed on their whaling ships.

The word harpoon is said to come from the Basque *arpoi*, but this was probably derived from the French *harper* – to seize or grapple – which may in turn have come from the Latin *harpago*, a hook or grappling iron. Sir Clements Markham, who travelled through the Basque provinces in search of whaling relics, found a harpoon with a movable barb that was held closed by a ring. As the harpoon entered the whale's body the ring was pushed back and the barb allowed to open and grip the flesh. Similar harpoons were once used by the Norwegians in hunting belugas, and this is further evidence for a link between them and the Basques. Movable barb harpoons must, however, have been abandoned at some stage in the mainstream of whaling history because fixed barb harpoons were later in general use, until the toggle-iron was invented by an American blacksmith in 1848; although Eskimos also invented a form of movable barb harpoon.

The number of whales killed by the Basques does not seem to have been very great. In the sixteenth century the men of Lequeitio killed, on average, only one or two whales a year, but in 1538 they killed six whales. Compared with the numbers killed in modern whaling (about 60,000 whales were killed each year during the 1950s), the Basques would seem to have taken a negligible number of whales, but during the middle of the seventeenth century the catches decreased and right whales became rare along the Biscayan coast.

We have no idea how abundant were the Biscayan right whales when the Basques started their operations, but it is surprising that such a comparatively small industry could have so severely affected their numbers. It is not impossible that over the course of three or four centuries the whales learned to avoid the coasts and took to a new route farther out to sea.

Until the modern whaling fleets started to scour the oceans and kill whales by the thousand, it was often suggested that the decreasing success of a particular fishery was due to the whales changing their habits. Melville appeared to be convinced that sperm whales were not decreasing in numbers but had changed their habits. He claimed that at one time they lived solitarily or in small schools but, under pressure of hunting, banded in very large, but well-scattered, convoys and so were less frequently encountered. Scammon describes how the gray whales started giving the shores of California a wide berth a few years after intensive whaling started there.

Whatever the cause of the whales' disappearance from the Bay of Biscay, the Basque whalers had to travel farther afield, although porpoises and the occasional right whale were killed in the Bay of Biscay until the late nineteenth century. In the sixteenth century Basques and others were fishing for cod on the Grand Banks of Newfoundland and the news soon spread that there was an abundance of whales there. The Basque whalers were quick to take advantage of the new whale-fishing ground and in 1578 Anthony Parkhurst saw twenty to thirty Basque whaling ships off Newfoundland. The first English whaling expedition did not set out until 1594, and it worked in the Gulf of St Lawrence.

This was the period when western Europeans started to thrust out across the Atlantic on voyages of discovery. Starting with Columbus's voyage to the New World in 1492, the Portuguese and Spanish followed towards the warmer regions of the Caribbean and South America, seeking a passage to India and China. At the same time the northern nations were sending expeditions in search of the North-west Passage to the same destination. Sebastian Cabot set out from Bristol and reached Labrador in 1496 and he attempted to find the North-west Passage in 1517. He was followed by the Englishmen Jonas Poole in 1583 and John Davis in 1585. In 1596 the Dutch explorer Barendz discovered Spitzbergen, and Hudson sailed into the bay that received his name in 1610. The North-west Passage was not finally revealed until 1850 but, as the Portuguese and Spaniards discovered the riches of tropical America, so the English and Dutch explorers came home with stories of seas teeming with whales. These were Greenland right whales and entrepreneurs of both countries, together with Danes, Germans and others, soon set sail to the northern seas, where fortunes were made, lives lost and adventures experienced, the equal of those recounted from the better known and warmer climate of tropical America.

At first the key to success at whaling lay in hiring Basques to do the catching and cutting up, but these pioneers disappeared from the scene as their employers learnt to perform these intricate tasks themselves. The ships used in these voyages were only 30–60 metres long and carried crews of up to fifty. Richard Hakluyt gives advice on the fitting out of a whaling ship in his *Collection of Voyages*. Among the more noteworthy items to be carried are one hundred and fifty hogsheads (43,640 litres) of cider, four tunnes (4,655 litres) of wine and four and a half kintals of bread for each man, as well as harping irons (harpoons), javelins great and small, tackles, hooks, hogsheads, kettles, furnaces 'to melt the Whale in', ladles, '3 pairs of boots great and strong, for them that shall cut the Whale' and five pinnases (pinnaces). The crew should include 'five men to strike with harping irons (one for each pinnase), two cutters of whale, five coopers and a purser or two'. The 'cutters of whale', known as specksioneers or inspecksioneers from the Dutch *Specksnyder* – fat-cutter – were important men and later became the chief harpooners as well as overseers of the processing of the carcase, but the office eventually lapsed.

The first English ship to go whaling in the Arctic seas, as opposed to the rather warmer seas of Newfoundland and Iceland, set out from Hull in 1611. It had a profitable voyage and more ships followed in later years. In 1612 Dutch ships joined in the chase and the two countries were rivals for the next two hundred years, with the Dutch leading at first but eventually losing out as England became dominant both economically and politically. This was a golden age of whaling, perhaps rivalled only by the early years of whaling in the Antarctic, where there were similar hordes of whales to be had for the taking. It was the time when whalebone fetched the oft-quoted price of £2,250 a ton, and each whale yielded one and a half tons of whalebone and twenty-five tons of oil.

The seventeenth-century whalers worked around the coasts of Jan Mayen and Spitzbergen, known as the Greenland fishery because Spitzbergen was then known as East Greenland. There was considerable rivalry among the whalers. The Muscovy Company, a body of merchants similar to the

Hudson's Bay Company, but trading with Russia, sent ships around the North Cape into the White Sea and obtained a royal charter granting monopoly of the whaling rights in northern waters. This was challenged by other English companies as well as by foreigners, and considerable effort and money were wasted in sending armed ships to protect the whalers. Eventually it was realized that there were enough whales for all and the coast of Spitzbergen was divided between the interested nations.

The profits from the Greenland fishery could be enormous; one whale paid for outfitting a ship and a ship might catch over fifty whales in a season, sometimes abandoning the carcases through lack of space or time. On the other hand, ships sometimes came home empty or failed to return altogether. Again, their cargo and equipment might be forcibly removed by ships of another nation because monopolies, or the division of the coastline, were only effective when supported by power. Sometimes the English came back rich and sometimes the Dutch or French were winners. Occasionally insult was added to injury, as when an English captain complained that one Cornelius de Cock said that 'our King of England was a Scotsman, and that his picture stood at Flushinge with an emptie purse by his side'. The English seem to have been generally unpopular because they ignored the unwritten 'Greenland Law' – that a whale belonged solely to the ship that was fastened to it – and behaved 'as Lords of the Ocean and all its inhabitants'.

A handful of accounts of Greenland whaling appeared during the seventeenth century. The procedures that they describe had already been established for up to five centuries, having been learned from the Basques, and apart from the quaint language used the authors could have been sailing in the same ships as Melville, Bullen or Murphy. A high degree of efficiency in the use of rowing boats, hand harpoons and lances for the killing of whales must therefore have been attained at an early stage in the history of whaling, and there was almost no way in which it could be improved until the introduction of harpoon guns and steam catchers.

In 1671 Frederic Marten set sail for Spitzbergen in the whale-ship *Jonas in the Whale*. On his arrival at the whaling-grounds he saw many ships which when passing 'hailed one another, crying *Holla*! and asked each other how many fish they had caught'. This was another area in which the English earned the scorn of other nations. It was their habit to ask the other crew how many whales they had caught, then to claim a total two or three in excess of the others. The habit of 'speaking a ship' or 'gamming' became a convention with whalers and in the nineteenth century two ships might heave-to while the crews went aboard each others ships to chat and compare adventures. Except for the rare call at a port for stores or repairs, gamming was the only contact the whalers might have with the outside world for three or four years on end.

The whalers that Frederic Marten observed were chasing their quarry in boats that held six men: a harpooner, a steersman and four oarsmen. They rowed up to the whale, the harpooner stood up and thrust his weapon into the whale's back. The harpoon had two tines, each with a sharp leading edge but blunt behind like an axehead, so that it cut easily into the whale's flesh but would not pull out. The harpoon was not intended to kill or even disable the whale, but merely fastened it to the boat. When it struck the whale's back the heavy wooden shaft came away, leaving a forerunner of the best pliable hemp rope running back to the boat where it was fastened to coils of heavier tarred rope.

As soon as the whale was harpooned, or 'struck' (the harpoon was said to be 'planted' not thrown) the oarsmen slipped their oars and turned to face the bow. Great care was taken as the line rushed out to see that it ran freely without kinks or loops that might catch, and that it ran straight over the bows so that the boat was not pulled over. In the centre of the boat was a stout post, the stave, later known as the bollard or, to the Americans, the loggerhead. The line passed around the stave to slow its running, the friction being so great that it had to be continually dampened with sea water to prevent the wood scorching.

By slowing the rate at which the whale drew out the line by wrapping it around the stave, and by hauling in any slack, they brought the boat gradually towards the whale, giving the harpooner a chance to kill it with lance-thrusts. The lances were 2-metre steel rods, tipped with sharp blades and fitted into a 4-metre wooden shaft. As soon as the boat closed with the whale the harpooner thrust the lance into its body, worked it about, churning and plunging to enlarge the wound and strike a vital spot. His aim was to place the lance into the whale's back and to penetrate the great blood vessels, causing the whale to spout blood, a sure sign that its end was near.

With the thrashing of the whale in its agony and the movement of the boat the harpooner had little chance to aim and place the lance where he wanted. He had to stab as and when he could, calling out to his crew to row forward to the whale or back quickly to avoid the lashing flukes, while the steersman manipulated the long steering oar, spinning the boat to keep the bow towards the whale.

The physical and mental stress on the boat's crew can be imagined. Firstly, they had probably spent hours in an open boat on the icy sea, because there might be anything from fifteen minutes to forty hours between the harpooning and the killing of a whale. They might be towed out of sight of their parent ship and be lost in darkness or fog. Then, over and above such discomforts that can befall any mariner, their main aim was to bring their boat as close as possible to one of the largest animals that has ever existed, and drive it mad with pain from repeated stab wounds. They must have been continually conscious that every centimetre of harpoon line hauled back into the boat brought them nearer the danger of the stricken whale. William Scoresby summed up this danger in a letter to Sir Joseph Banks:

> In the Tail lays the whole strength of the whale, it is the fisherman's [whaler's] greatest fear, the power and the weight so great that boats are stove, upset, perhaps completely severed in two, sometimes thrown quite out of the water, or crushed to atoms beneath the stroke. The Tyro shrinks with fear, and views with terror the mighty member waving above his head, and cracking like a whip but 10 times louder which sometimes tempts him to leap into the sea to seek refuge from the impending blow.

It is incredible that men should have pitted themselves against these monstrous creatures with such frail equipment and at such close quarters. Rarely has man taken on fights with animals at such heavy odds. It calls to mind knights-errant charging fiery dragons or Masai warriors grabbing the tails of lions while their companions attack with spears, but the knights and warriors battled for honour and prestige while whalers toiled for a low wage. The most that a whaleman could hope for when his boat was wrecked was that he might be picked up, shocked and frozen, by another boat.

It was the custom for the other crews to wait nearby and lend extra lines if the whale was pulling strongly (one whale is recorded as pulling out over 9,000 metres of line) and to help tow the carcase back. For the killing of the whale was not the end of the operation. The tail had to be cut off or lashed up to make towing easier and the carcase laboriously rowed back to the ship where it had to be cut up before the weather deteriorated or the body decayed.

It is hard to find out just how hazardous was the catching of whales from open boats. Danger was always present but luck and skill must have lessened the risk or whaling would never have been a worthwhile proposition. Between 1669 and 1778 the Dutch whalers lost about four per cent of their men which, considering the hazards to life in those days, does not seem to be a particularly high proportion. On the other hand, there was immense suffering among men whose ships were ripped and sunk in the Arctic ice pack, or caught and frozen in for the winter, especially when compounded by frostbite and scurvy. To quote one case, the *Advice* drifted into Sligo Bay, Ireland, with only seven men left from a crew of sixty-nine, and three of these were half dead from their privations.

In the early years of the Greenland whale-fishery the ships operated close inland. The whales were towed to the shore where each nation had set up a factory for stripping the carcases of their blubber and whalebone. In 1622 the Dutch constructed the 'village' of Smeerenburg (Dutch *smeeren* – to melt, *burg* – town), sending building materials out from Holland and erecting a cluster of huts behind the shore. Smeerenburg expanded into an Arctic metropolis. Each whaling company had its own slipway, boilers and warehouses and there was accommodation for upwards of 15,000 men. In the wake of the whalers came tradesmen to sell tobacco, spirits and fresh bread, and there was even a church and a fort.

The business of boiling, or trying-out, the blubber was

conducted on the production-line principle. As the blubber was hauled ashore any remaining pieces of flesh were stripped off by the waterside man, who stood up to his knees in the sea. He also cut the strips of blubber into lumps weighing about 90 kilograms. Each lump was carried up the shore by wheelbarrow and cut into smaller pieces. They were placed on a chopping block made of the tough flesh of whales' flukes and sliced into fine shreds. These were put into a large copper boiler mounted on a brick furnace – the tryworks. The blubber was heated and the mixture of oil and tissue that resulted was put through a sieve and the oil poured into a series of three vats half full of water to cool it down. The vats were mounted at different levels and were connected by spouts so that the oil ran from the top vat to the bottom vat, being progressively cooled, while impurities sank into the water. Meanwhile, the jaws of the whale were being stripped of their whalebone, each blade being scrubbed with sand and scraped to remove the tissue that secured it in the mouth.

The thick, viscid oil retrieved from the blubber was called train-oil (from the Dutch *traan* – tear or drop). It was used for lighting, as a lubricant, and – as techniques advanced – in the manufacture of soap and paint and the processing of jute. Glycerine was extracted to make explosives and in the early nineteenth century several English towns were lit by gas made from train-oil. The oil and whalebone were sent home in barrels either in the whale-ships or, when the Spitzbergen whaling was at its peak, in merchant ships that came out in ballast.

The peak of the Spitzbergen inshore or bay whaling came about 1636. After that catches declined as the whales either became scarce or changed their habits. The whale-ships had then to pursue them out to sea or into the pack ice. The splash and hiss of the waves breaking over the ice floes drowned the noise of the approaching boats and made stalking the whales easier, but the floes brought a new hazard for the whalers because a harpooned whale might try to escape by swimming under the ice. The harpooner had an awkward decision to make if this happened because, to save his boat, he had to cut his line thereby losing not only the whale but also his harpoon and many yards of rope. One trick, unpleasant for the crew, was to leave the line fastened to the boat, jump into the sea and wait to be picked up by another boat. The whale had then to tow the boat as well as the rope, which itself offers a surprising resistance to being dragged through the water. Eventually, it was hoped, the whale would die and the boat would act as a buoy to mark its position.

During the second half of the seventeenth century Smeeren-burg and the other shore stations declined in importance because the distance that the whales had to be towed became too great. The blubber was now stripped while the whale lay alongside the ship, and was cut into pieces called flitches and stored in barrels on board. The blubber was tried-out at a shore station or kept in the barrels until the return home.

A few French ships were fitted out with tryworks on the deck so that the blubber could be boiled at sea, but too many ships caught fire for the practice to become popular. Blubber continued to be brought back to Europe in barrels – and, later, in iron tanks – until the nineteenth century, despite the fact that the Americans successfully used shipboard tryworks when sperm-whaling in the tropics and hunting right whales in the north.

Flensing a whale alongside a ship was a difficult task, particularly if the sea was rough. The whale was tied to the side of the ship, head facing sternwards, on the port side. Two boats were moored outside the whale to act as a platform from which the specksioneer or harpooners cut great furrows in the blubber with long-handled knives. If there was a sea running, the movement of the ship, whale and boats made the operation precarious and the men often wore spiked boots to give them a firm grip on the slippery skin of the whale.

The whale lay on its side during this operation and large rectangles of blubber, each weighing about a ton, were lifted from the body. The harpooner severed the sheets of blubber from the underlying tissue and they were lifted by ropes that ran from the cradle, a kind of crow's nest on the mast. As the sheet was drawn up, two men pulled it in with hooks while two more cut it into pieces about 100 square centimetres and removed the adhering flesh. These men were called krengers as they removed the flesh or 'kreng' which would cause the blubber to ferment if left on. The squares were dragged to the starboard side of the ship and laid, skin-side down, on the bench. The blubber was stripped away from the skin, minced and pushed into a trough running behind the bench. The final task was to push the oily mess along the trough and down a canvas bag into the hold where it was packed into barrels. The cutting up and packing of the blubber was known as 'making-off', from the Dutch *afmaaken* – to finish or complete.

When the blubber had been stripped from one side of the carcase, the whalebone was cut out and the whale turned over so that the rest of the blubber could be removed. Finally the body was cast off and allowed to float away.

After the peak of the Spitzbergen fishery was reached in 1636 a decline set in. Fewer ships brought home full cargoes, although at the end of the century the catch around Spitzbergen was still about 2,000 whales a year. By 1720, however, there were no more whales left in the area. Smeerenburg and the other factories fell into ruins and Spitzbergen became deserted except for occasional visits from explorers. The whalers had moved to new hunting grounds; along the ice edge to the east of Greenland, in Baffin Bay and up the Davis Strait. This new fishery started in 1719 when Dutch ships entered the Davis Straits. It flourished throughout the eighteenth century and continued into the twentieth century. When it started the Dutch were still supreme and the English whaling industry had begun a temporary decline.

To bolster an industry that brought in such essential materials as train-oil and whalebone but suffered from the attacks of foreign privateers, the British Government introduced a bounty system, paying towards the cost of fitting out whaling-ships. In 1748 £1 was paid for each ton of the ship and this was doubled in 1750. In 1777, for instance, the *Volunteer* of Whitby received a bounty of £800, equal to one ninth of the value of her cargo. She had caught five whales that yielded sixty-five tons of train-oil, worth £1,300 and between four and five tons of whalebone, worth £2,300. In later years the bounty was given for a different reason. The whale-ships were seen as nurseries to supply the Royal Navy with seasoned sailors. They were given £50 for each boat they could lower after whales.

Throughout the seventeenth century wars had their effect on

shipping. During the French wars and the American Revolution, English ships suffered from attacks by privateers and at the close of the century the Royal Navy had taken to escorting the whaling fleet to and from the Arctic. The Dutch fleet suffered at the hands of the British and French navies and in 1798 a British convoying force captured the Dutch ships and never again was Holland a leader among whaling nations. The hunt for Greenland right whales in Arctic waters fell increasingly to the British and Americans, whose exploits and fortunes are described in Chapter 12.

10 | The Sperm-Whalers

AT the same time as the British whalers started their hunt for whales in Arctic waters, colonists in the New World began to harvest the rich crop of whales that travelled close to the shores of Newfoundland and New England. The beginnings of this whale-fishery are open to question. It seems certain that stranded whales offered the same bounty as they did on the other side of the Atlantic. The proceeds were divided among those that had helped cut up and boil the blubber on an improvised tryworks on the shore, with a proportion going to the church.

From the dismembering of such whales to the harpooning and towing ashore of whales that appeared close to the land was only a short step. The uncertainty lies in the manner by which the colonists became acquainted with whaling techniques. It has often been suggested that the English settlers copied the methods of the Indians, who certainly knew how to pursue whales at the time of the colonists' arrival. However, Edouard Stackpole, who has written a very thorough history of American whaling in *The Sea-Hunters*, contends that it is the Indians who took over European methods to improve on their primitive techniques of harassing and killing. The Europeans probably adapted some of the Indians' equipment such as 'drogues' – balks of timber attached to the whale-line to brake the whale's escape, and they definitely employed Indians as lookouts and crewmen. Although it cannot be proved from documentary evidence that the European settlers brought with them their own methods of whale-hunting, it seems clear that this was so from the similarity of the whaling gear and techniques of the American whalers with those of the early Basques and contemporary European whalers working in Arctic waters.

The first whaling expeditions around the Nantucket coast,

the birthplace of American whaling, and from the colonies at New York and Connecticut, were quite simple. Small boats patrolled the shore, staying away from home for only a couple of weeks and dragging their whales ashore to try-out the blubber on the beach. The whales so caught were humpbacks, right whales and, it seems, the gray whale, species which travel close to the shore when migrating. The sperm whales, which were to become the main quarry for American whalers and on which their prosperity and reputation were founded, kept farther offshore. They were not hunted until a whale-ship was accidentally blown out to sea in 1712, about a century after the start of the colonists' pursuit of whales.

The captain, Christopher Hussey, found himself among a school of sperm whales, killed one and towed it home. Sperm whale oil had already been obtained from stranded carcases and its excellence was appreciated, so the New Englanders readily followed Hussey's lead and set out after sperm whales on six-week cruises, bringing the blubber home in barrels. From this chance encounter the great sperm-whale fishery was set in being. It flourished until the early part of the nineteenth century, when whalers were scouring every corner of the oceans for their quarry, and lingered on for another century until modern steam catchers equipped with heavy harpoon guns took over. It now survives in the Azores and other out-of-the-way places where the whales are killed for local use.

Whaling developed rapidly on the New England coast and there was a boom in the latter half of the seventeenth century which extended into the eighteenth. From the island of Nantucket whaling spread to other harbours and ports, such as Martha's Vineyard, Salem, New Bedford and Sag Harbour. At the same time the Dutch colonists were hunting whales from New York, and the French at Quebec were employing Basque harpooners. The oil and whalebone were much in demand in the expanding colonies and also formed a very valuable source of revenue when exported to England, where an increasing population and developing industries demanded more oil for lighting and lubrication. Train-oil and whalebone from right whales, sperm-oil and candles made from spermaceti received high prices. Furthermore, the British Government granted concessions to the whaling industry. Bounties were given to whalers on each side of the Atlantic, as both the New England whalers and those sailing from British ports needed compensation from the depredations of foreign privateers who found the cumbersome whale-ships an easy and profitable prey.

The shore-fishery for whalebone whales gradually declined during the early part of the eighteenth century, but sperm-whaling on the high seas burgeoned as the whalers discovered new fishing grounds in both the North and the South Atlantic. The sperm whale lacked the valuable whalebone of the hump-back and right whales but its blubber oil had valuable properties of its own and there was also the spermaceti from the head and the lucky chance of finding ambergris.

In their early voyages the American whalers followed the example of their European counterparts in tearing the blubber off the whale as it lay alongside the ship and stowing it in barrels. Trying-out was conducted on land when the voyage was over but, as the ships stayed away from port for longer periods, it became necessary to treat the blubber immediately so that its bulk was reduced and spoilage was prevented. European whalers had soon been deterred from erecting try-works on board after several ships had caught fire and im-mediate trying-out was less important on their short voyages in cold climates. For the Americans, with their long cruises in tropical waters, the situation was different; and they appear to have developed a practical shipborne tryworks without encountering any disasters.

The tryworks made a whaling vessel unmistakable. Sitting amidships, it appeared as a giant field-kitchen of brick bound with iron braces, 1·5 metres high and about 3 metres square, with two 900 litre pots set over a primitive furnace. Whaling ships were blunt and broad in the beam – 'built by the mile and cut off in lengths as you want 'em' – and the square tryworks, stout spars and all the paraphernalia of dealing with gigantic whale carcases added to the impression of a floating factory, so different from the graceful speedy clippers that quartered the same seas. For safety's sake the tryworks stood in a 30 centimetres deep tray of water which prevented the deck from scorching and catching fire. Over the furnace there stood iron flues to prevent the oil slopping into the furnace as the ship rolled and pitched. Surrounding the tryworks were the accessories of trying-out: a machine to cut up the blubber, a wooden vessel to hold the raw slices and a copper tank in which the oil stood to cool before being stowed in barrels.

The cutting-in of a sperm whale was conducted along the same lines as with a right whale. The whale was securely fastened to the ship's side and a 'cutting-in stage' of stout planks was rigged around it. A handrail helped to steady the officers as they attacked the carcase with long-handled 'spades', and ropes around their waists assured their safety. The first job was to cut off the head, severing it just behind the skull, a difficult job that involved careful dissection and manoeuvring of the huge weight of the whale.

First, a hole was cut in the blubber between one eye and one flipper. A large hook was inserted and the strain taken on the lifting tackle until the whale rolled on its side. A chain was passed around the lower jaw and raised, so that the whale rolled onto its back and the lower jaw could be cut off and lifted on board. The whale was then turned on the other side, cuts made in the head and chains passed through the snout to secure it. Then one of the most difficult manoeuvres was attempted. The chains holding the flukes and the body behind the eye were slacked off and the crew combined to haul in the tackle attached to the snout. This brought the whale into a vertical position, head uppermost, and the officers were able to cut around the base of the skull, the weight of the body assisting in tearing the flesh, until the neck bones were severed.

The head was left to float astern until the blubber had been dealt with, and, presumably, the crew had paused to relax from their mental and physical strain. A bald description of the removal of the head cannot convey the difficulties and dangers of the operation when a large sperm whale was being cut-in with a heavy sea running. The officers must have risked being swept off the stage, crushed by the whale or even severely gashed by their sharp tools at every turn, while the crew had to exert every sinew at the windlass to drag the carcase into position. According to accounts there were some whaling captains that did not allow their crews the luxury of a rest until the job of cutting-in was completely finished, not even allowing them to recover from the rigours of chasing the whale and towing it back to the ship before starting to cut-in. There was some necessity in this high-handed action as a whale could easily be lost if a storm blew up, so setting to naught the crew's earlier exertions.

After the head had been removed, the fluke chain was hauled tight again and the blubber was stripped off in a spiral sheet, the body rolling over and over as the tackle attached to the blubber behind the eye was taken in. The sheet of blubber was cut into 'blanket pieces' as it came aboard and these were stowed in the 'blubber room' below decks. Attention now returned to the head. If it was that of a small whale it was lifted on board by the exertions of the whole crew; if it was too large to be brought aboard it was secured to the side of the ship. The head of the sperm whale is the repository of the spermaceti, which is liquid at body temperature but solidifies as it cools. The lower part of the head was called the 'junk' and contained spermaceti in a matrix of tough, white fibres. The junk was cut off and put to one side for treatment later, while the upper part of the head – the 'case' – was opened to reveal a reservoir of pure spermaceti. This was baled into casks and the remains of the head thrown overboard to complete the process of cutting-in.

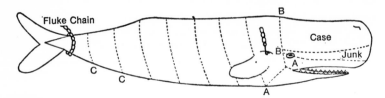

Figure 12 Cutting-in a sperm whale. A–A removes the jaw, B–B removes the head and the blubber is cut off in a strip from A–A to C–C.

There remained one task before the carcase was set free to drift away. According to Murphy, the officers thrust sharp cutting spades deep into the whale's guts in 'the rite of the whaleman's ultimate hope' and, withdrawing them, carefully smelt the blades for any trace of ambergris. This evil-smelling lumpy substance was an occasional bonus for the sperm-whalers. At one time it was thought to come only from sick sperm whales but it has now been found in the intestines of healthy whales. After exposure to the air ambergris loses its offensive odour and, until the gradual replacement by synthetics it was used, like musk and civet, as a base for perfumes. It fetched an extremely high price, once as high as £5 per ounce, and in 1912 a whaling company was saved from liquidation by the discovery of a 450 kilogram lump of ambergris which was sold for £23,000.

Ambergris has been of value since the ninth century when pieces were found cast up on the shore. It was used in medicines, to spice wines, and as an aphrodisiac, as well as being a base for perfumes. Its origin was unknown until 1724, and its function is still a mystery. At one time it was thought to be the equivalent of a pearl in an oyster – a special secretion for covering the sharp beaks of squids – but this notion has been discounted.

Once free of the carcase it was time for trying-out the blubber. The blanket pieces were brought up on deck and sliced into 'horse pieces' either with a two-handed knife or with a machine in which a knife rose and fell as a wheel was turned. The horse pieces were not cut into slices like a side of bacon but only deeply scored, leaving the skin at the back intact to hold the thin strips of blubber like the leaves of a coarse, oily book. Slicing the blubber into horse pieces allowed the oil to be rapidly cooked out.

The harpooners were in charge of the trying-out, throwing horse pieces into the large pots and ladling off the hot oil into a cooling tank. The process was extremely economical as the main fuel was scrap or fritters, the crisp, brown tissue that is the remains of horse pieces after the oil has been removed. It burns with a hot, clean flame and, to sailors on other ships, the sight of a whaling vessel at work after nightfall must have presented an eerie sight as it drifted under a minimum of canvas with the wheel lashed down, the toiling crew and the rigging lit up by the glare of the tryworks fire. To the crew of the whaler trying-out was a messy business, as the decks and their clothes became saturated with oil. The scuppers were blocked before cutting-in started so that the oil swilling over the deck could not escape. One of the last chores was to mop up this oil and add it to the rest in the trypots. When all the blubber had been disposed of, the decks and the men were thoroughly washed down and the barrels of oil were taken below and securely stowed.

At the home port the oil was subjected to further processing. It was cleaned of dirt and oil and left to stand for the winter to become a near-solid 'black cake', which was squeezed in a press to produce 'winter-oil'. This would not freeze in the winter. Second and third pressings gave lower quality 'spring' and 'summer' oil. The residue was used in the manufacture of candles. The fine spermaceti wax was also used in cosmetics and medicines.

As they toiled among the heaps of blubber the whaling crew could comfort themselves with the thought that each barrel filled brought their home-coming nearer and more money into their pockets. Throughout the eighteenth century the New England sperm-whalers prospered. The price of sperm-oil had risen to £40 a ton by 1770 and in that year, Nantucket alone had a fleet of over one hundred ships, whose catch was valued at £150,000. But five years later the American whaling industry was hit by the first of several disasters.

The British Government, which had once supported the American whalers with bounties, now started to act against them. In 1766 a duty was placed on oil and whalebone imported from America, while bounties were still given to whalers sailing from Great Britain. Yet when the Americans' dissatisfaction with the British Government boiled over into the War of Independence, the whaling ports were still closely bound to the home country. Nantucket became a haven for loyalists and the whalers were caught in a crossfire. The revolutionaries on the mainland refused to trade with the people on the island of Nantucket and British privateers waited to snap up any ships that came their way and force their crews to serve as British seamen.

By diplomacy and cunning, the Nantucketers attempted to continue their trade in whales throughout the war, but by the end only thirty-five whaling ships remained of the one hundred and thirty-two that existed in 1775. Rebel ports suffered worse: in retaliation for the activities of their privateers, New Bedford and other villages were attacked and looted by the British, and their ships were destroyed. After the war the

Nantucketers found the British market still closed by a formidable tariff wall and attempts were made to trade with the French.

Despite these political troubles the whaling industry flourished and the whalers pushed farther across the oceans in search of their quarry. At first they sailed to the Caribbean and the Gulf of Mexico. The 'Brazil Banks' fishery started in 1744 and in 1765 American whalers were crossing the Atlantic to the Western Islands, as they called the Azores, and to the coast of Africa. A rich fishing ground was also found around the Falkland Islands and the River Plate, but the real break-through was the discovery in the mid-nineteenth century of whaling grounds in the Indian and Pacific Oceans. This led to the peak of American sperm-whaling and the four- or five-year voyages experienced by Melville and Bullen.

Ironically the two main discoveries in the Pacific were made by British ships, although one at least was manned by Nantucketers who had moved to England after the War of Independence. In 1788 the *Emelia*, belonging to the Enderby brothers whose company combined exploration with whaling, sailed around Cape Horn into the Pacific and hunted in what later became known as the Chile Coast or 'On-shore' fishing grounds. In 1819, another British ship, the *Syren*, started the exploitation of the 'Coast of Japan' as the north-west Pacific was called by whalemen.

Fishing in the last of the major sperm-whaling grounds to be discovered was known as 'cruising down the line', a phrase that referred to sailing the seas bordering the equator. In theory a Pacific cruise was idyllic, with the tropical sun beating down and palm-laden Pacific Islands, such as Hawaii and Fiji, to visit, but in practice it was probably as unpleasant as buffeting through the stormy seas of higher latitudes. The sun's heat boiled the pitch that caulked the deck timbers, making the crowded, airless fo'c'sle a Black Hole. Visits to Pacific Islands usually meant hard work filling water casks and cutting fire-wood. Even the chance of going ashore to get roaring drunk might be spoiled by unfriendly natives who made it necessary to fight off fleets of canoes with harpoon and lance.

The rigours and questionable delights of these long voyages, tedious although not monotonous, and broken only by the

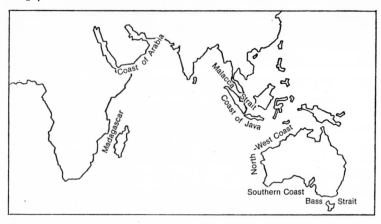

danger of storms and whale-catching, have been preserved in several books written by the men who took part. Some are a disappointment to anyone wishing to learn more about whaling. The author has often assumed that his readers are familiar with the techniques of sailing as well as whaling and

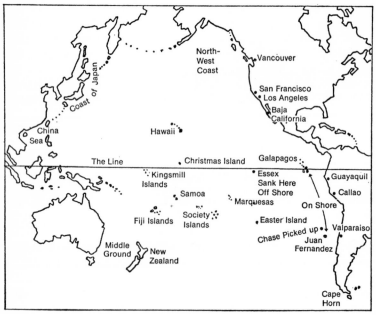

Figure 13 The main sperm-whaling grounds of the world.

becomes expansive only when dealing with topics unrelated to whaling, such as a visit to an island or a fight amongst the crew. For example, Nelson Cole Haley, who ran away from home to go a-whaling, assumes his readers are sailors and describes two ships meeting for a 'gam' in *Whale Hunt*:

Standing along until the other ship bore about two points forward of our lee beam, our wheel was put hard up and the yards squared. As the ship got before the wind and pointed her flying jibboom for the mainmast, he at the same time hauled aback his main-topsail, and being not far apart, we soon came within speaking distance.

Without a knowledge of sailing this is meaningless but it is, in fact, a ticklish manœuvre in which one ship headed straight for the other then, just as collision seemed inevitable, swung away to pass behind the other's stern, so close that the captains could exchange news in normal voices.

Frank Bullen, on the other hand, who was once a London street-arab and who went whaling more by mistake than intention, is at pains to describe the technicalities of life on a whale-ship, so his narrative comes to life and the reader can readily visualize the scenes and activities. A further difference between *Whale Hunt* and Bullen's *Cruise of the Cachalot* is that Bullen, who had had experience on merchant ships, was sympathetic towards the greenhorns in the whaling crew, whereas Haley, the professional, is scathing about their short-comings. It was usual for a whale-ship to carry in its crew inexperienced members who were either city riffraff or country lads from land-bound states. To them, the sea itself was a novelty, let alone the experiences of climbing along the yards way above a bucking deck to reef a sail, or rowing a frail boat right up to a thrashing sperm whale. One can easily imagine the terror of the sea-sick men as they attempted to carry out incomprehensible but forcefully expressed orders. The saying that a soldier has to fear his officers more than the enemy must also have applied to whalers.

The raw crews received their shake-down on crossing the Atlantic from New England to the Azores. They were assigned to watches for working the ship and to crews for the boats while the experienced men broke out the whaling gear and fitted out the boats, and masthead lookouts swept the sea for tell-tale spouts, crying 'She blows' to rouse the crew and send the captain leaping up the rigging.

In parentheses, it should be noted here that the chroniclers of American sperm-whaling often differ in their description and occasionally criticize each other openly. It has been pointed out that Herman Melville's 'There she blows!' is too long-winded a cry for an excited lookout. He was more likely to sing out 'She blows!' or 'Ah blows!' or just 'Blows!' Robert Cushman Murphy says that the men of the brig *Daisy* shouted 'Blo-o-o-o-o-o-ws!' and 'For spermaceti they go plum crazy, and sing at the top of their lungs'. The whole crew joins in as they rush about getting ready to lower the boats, so that the ship is filled with a monotone chorus. It is interesting that the present-day Azores whalers, who use the equipment and techniques of the American sperm-whalers, sing out '*Bloz!*' More importantly, William Williams of *One Whaling Family*, points out that Melville's exciting description of the boats being rowed after the whale with the officers bellowing exhortation 'just never happened'. The whole art of 'going on' a whale consisted of sneaking up without it being frightened or 'gallied'. To this end, the boats sailed to within one hundred metres of the whale, then a change was made to paddling. Lowering the sail and mast or shipping the oars was a ticklish task that had to be accomplished without knocking the hull of the boat and alerting the whale. Whalers only rowed onto a whale when it was about to sound and speed was the prime consideration.

However, to take one step back, after a whale was sighted the boats were swung out in readiness for the order to lower away as the ship closed with its quarry. The typical American whaling boat was an excellent sea-boat, pointed at each end, 6–9 metres long and 1·8 metres in beam. Until the middle of the nineteenth century, whale-boats were clinker-built with overlapping planks, but carvel-built boats with flush planking became popular because they ran through the water with less noise. In the bow there was a groove through which the line ran, held in place by a pin. One metre back was the 'clumsy-cleat' or 'thighboard', a thwart with a notch in which the harpooner braced his leg to steady himself. In the middle of the boat were five thwarts for the oarsmen, then another clumsy-cleat for the steersman who worked the long steering oar, and the loggerhead, a 20 centimetre post around which the line ran. A surprising amount of gear fitted into the boat: six harpoons, three lances, mast, sails, two tubs with 550 metres of line, a drogue for slowing down a running whale, hatchet, bailer, boathook and grapnel for securing the dead whale, keg with lantern, matches and emergency food, and so on.

As the boats set after the whale, two harpoons were attached to the line and rested in a crotch for immediate use. The officer in charge stood in the stern and guided his boat onto the whale. In this he was assisted from the ship, which was manned by a skeleton crew who gave signals in the form of flags hoisted or sails rearranged. For instance 'Whales ahead of ship' was signalled by lowering the flying jib and 'Whales between the boats' by raising flags at the fore and main mastheads.

To approach within harpooning distance, about 5 metres, the officer had to approach head-on – 'going on head and head' – or from behind – 'going on the flukes' – so that the whale did not see him. At the crucial moment, he pushed on the long steering oar to swing bow-on to the whale, the harpoon was darted, and a quick backstroke with the paddles lifted the boat clear.

The harpooner had little time to take aim and dart, but the harpoon had to go behind the head to avoid the skull and, for preference, it had to enter the arched back. If the back was depressed when the harpoon struck, the weapon was likely to be thrown out when the back arched and the wound enlarged. William Scoresby tells of a harpoon that was thrown clear into the air as the whale arched its back, but landed again point first and struck firmly into the whale which, in due course, was captured.

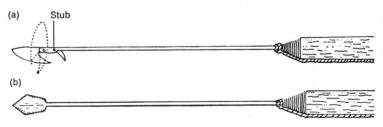

Figure 14 Toggle-iron harpoon (a) showing the movement of the barb, and (b) hand lance (modified from Scammon).

To hold firm, the harpoon had to penetrate the blubber, leaving its wooden pole behind, and fasten firmly in the underlying muscles. It was not unusual for a poorly thrown

11. A whale-catcher steams past the hills of South Georgia. Note the high, flared bows, the catwalk running from the bridge and the crow's nest

12. The factory at Grytviken. A whale is being dismembered on the plan and another floats offshore

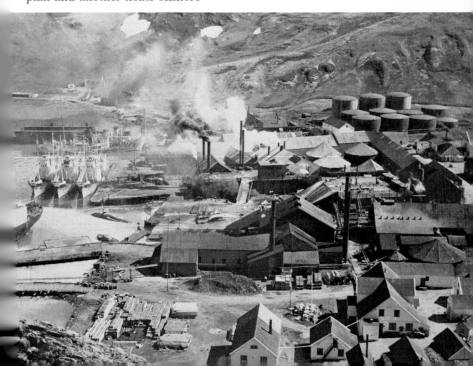

13. Japanese flensers make the first cuts in a fin whale with long-handled knives. The catcher behind them has its gun loaded

14. The plan at Hvalfordur, Iceland, showing a sei whale stripped of its blubber, which lies in strips to the left. The steam saw for cutting up bones is on the right

harpoon to draw, and often a second was thrown for extra security immediately after the first. An improved harpoon, the toggle iron, was invented by James Temple, a negro blacksmith of New Bedford, in 1848. The single barb was mounted on a pivot and held closed by a stub of wood, which shattered as it entered the whale and allowed the barb to swing out.

The whale's reaction to harpooning was usually to sound, taking 180–360 metres of line, then to charge off at the surface. As the line sang out it was essential to see that no kinks or loops appeared that could whip a man overboard or tear off a limb. Yet at this stage a most alarming manœuvre took place. The officer known as the boatheader left his steering oar and swapped places with the harpooner or boatsteerer, hopping from thwart to thwart. Melville considered this a foolish and needless custom, yet Professor Dakin found that it had persisted when he visited Twofold Bay in Australia in 1932, just as this relic of the old sperm-whaling days was about to close. As far as he could gather the swap-over was carried out because one man was a specialist with the harpoon and the other knew how to use a lance. Apparently one man could not be expected to do both. However, Azores whalers of the present day, who learned whaling from the Americans, do not bother to change places in the boat, neither did the British whalers.

If greenhorns were lucky they were able to practise these manœuvres on pilot whales or blackfish. The body blubber from these small cetaceans was hardly worth collecting but that from the head, particularly from the melon, was thirty times more valuable. Each animal gave 20–25 litres of very fine oil which was used as a lubricant in watches and other delicate machinery and at one time the flesh was salted or dried and traded for fresh food. After experience with blackfish, the greenhorns might not be so stricken with terror on meeting a sperm whale, but it was often necessary for the officer to keep a close check on his crew to prevent them jumping overboard, to everybody's jeopardy, and if there happened to be a series of accidents the crews sometimes became too scared even to man the boats.

After the whale had been harpooned and had set off on its blind chase, things became more orderly for the moment. The

5

whale-boat was towed willy-nilly through the waves in what was known as a Nantucket sleigh ride. The crew, meanwhile, exerted themselves to pull in the straining line until the bow was near enough – 'wood to blackskin' – for the boatheader to thrust in his lance. If the boat could not be brought sufficiently near for this, the boatheader might try 'pitch-poling' – tossing the lance like a caber and drawing it back on a line. He could also try to slow a strong whale by 'spading the flukes' – cutting at the small of the tail with a boat-spade, an instrument like a giant chisel with a 2 metre handle. Spading cut the tendons linking the flukes with the propulsive muscles – throwing the whale out of gear, as it were – and severed large veins so the whale bled to death.

At last the whale would go into its death throes, or flurry, heralded by its spouting blood. 'Its chimney's on fire' was the cry as the boat's crew was drenched in a fine red mist. Then the gigantic animal would thrash in circles, rearing its head and crashing its tail down, until it finally rolled on its side in a welter of foam – 'fin out'.

11 | The Decline of the Sperm-Whalers

In the heyday of sperm-whaling the grounds were often so crowded with whale-ships that their crews had to compete for the whales. Boats from two or more ships might chase one whale and the prize went to the crew that first got its harpoon in, but if these pulled out the whale was once more fair game for anyone. Sometimes two ships 'mated', cruising together, but well spaced, to increase the area covered by the look-outs, and co-operating in the killing of whales. The accounts of whaling in this period give the impression that the Americans had a monopoly of sperm-whaling, but other nations also participated. Nevertheless, the Americans were the most successful, as shown by one instance in which boats from the United States, England, France and Portugal chased the same whale during a flat calm. The Americans got the first harpoon in because, it was said, the habit of American boatheaders was to use one hand to push the oar of the stroke oarsman while working the steering oar with the other.

The peak of the New England whaling came in 1846, at a time when whalers were sending barrels of oil home by merchant ships before returning fully laden themselves, but before the peak period the industry had weathered one more crisis: the second destruction of the whaling fleet by the British Navy. Prior to this there had been an undeclared war with France in which more ships than ever were lost to privateers. Then in 1812 a war broke out between the Americans and the Canadians, the latter comprising French, British and Red Indians. Apart from the campaigns on land, the Royal Navy blockaded Nantucket and other whaling ports. News of the war was slow in reaching the ships, nearly of all which were cruising the Pacific whaling grounds, and they were captured, sometimes within sight of home, as they returned laden with oil from their long voyages. The population of Nantucket suffered severe privations during the blockade but such was the demand for whale products that soon after peace came in 1815 the industry was back in full swing. The Pacific 'off-shore' grounds and the Coast of Japan were opened up and exploited, while three species of whalebone whale, the bowhead or Greenland right whale, the humpback and the gray whale, were the objects of pursuit, leading the whalers down the coast of California and up through the Bering Straits.

The sperm whale boom did not last long for the New England ports and during the second half of the nineteenth century the industry slowly declined. This was not due to any one factor and the importance of any one cause is obscured by the influence of others. It is very likely that the stocks of sperm whales were being over-exploited, although this did not have an immediate effect because whalebone whales were taken in larger numbers. The introduction of kerosene, made from mineral oil for lighting in 1859, removed one of the main outlets for sperm-oil, but its introduction was gradual and there was still a demand for sperm-oil in the fast-growing industries of the nineteenth century. It was, for instance, still burnt in lighthouses and railway signalling lamps.

During the American Civil War, the New England whaling fleet was destroyed for the third and last time. Once again the whalers were unaware that a war was in progress and they were captured by Southern privateers as they sailed up the Atlantic. Later, the steam ship *Shenandoah* entered the Pacific to ravage Unionist shipping there and captured and burned thirty whale-ships. Eventually owners kept their ships lying idle in port for safety, or sold them. Then, finally, in 1861, forty whale-ships were gathered in New Bedford harbour and loaded with rocks. They set sail on November 16th as the 'Stone fleet' and were sunk at the entrance of Charleston harbour to foil privateers and blockade runners.

The inability of New England whalers to recover from this disaster, as they had from previous destructions, was probably due to the removal of the focal point of the whaling industry across the continent to San Francisco and, to a lesser extent, Honolulu. As most sperm whales were taken in the Pacific it was an obvious step to base the whaling fleet there, so cutting out the time-consuming journeys up and down the length of the Atlantic and around the dangerous Capes of Horn and Good Hope. The opening-up of the American West provided a nearby market and a bridgehead for export of oil to the rest of North America. San Francisco became the new centre of whaling, but this is not how the city is remembered. In 1849 the California gold-rush began and, although the owners of whaling-ships were provided with a new market, they had also to contend with vanishing crews who deserted in search of easier ways of getting rich.

Lust for gold was not necessary to drive a man to desert his ship. Apart from the professional 'career' whalers who hoped to become harpooners and officers who would eventually command their own ships, and the men shipped from the Azores, Cape Verde or the Pacific islands, the crew of a whaling-ship during the nineteenth century were unlikely to have entered this profession from choice.

Some whalers were seamen with such a poor reputation that no merchant ship would take them, which means that they must have been at the rock-bottom of society. Others signed on, like Bullen, because no other employment seemed forthcoming and debts were piling up. The keepers of low dockside lodgings would allow bills to run up, then recoup their losses, together with a commission, by supplying their erstwhile lodgers to a whaling-ship. Protest was kept to a minimum by ensuring that the draftees were soundly drunk. By the time they came round, it was too late – the ship was at sea and officers had the upper hand. Other men might find themselves being tricked into sailing on a whale-ship. Like Bullen, they might sign the ship's articles without knowing what sort of ship it was. They were then allowed to settle debts and collect their belongings under escort, and were taken out to the ship where it was riding at anchor to make escape impossible.

To keep this sort of crew in order needed strong discipline – commonly at the end of an officer's arm. Force was probably fairly administered for most of the time. Whaling officers worked their way up from the fo'c'sle, so they had to undergo a process of natural selection: only those men most capable of dominating subordinates survived to make the quarterdeck. Under such a regime a voyage might be bearable, provided that good whaling provided plenty of hard work and prospects of a quick return home, but a bullying officer, a failure to catch whales and a few mishaps made escape from the ship very desirable. San Francisco and the goldfields, or the Pacific islands with their promise of an idle life in a permissive society, were strong temptations. Melville, the arch-romantic of whaling, deserted his ship in the Marquesas and it was reckoned that few American whalers returned home in the same ship as they had set sail.

Added to the natural dangers of whaling and a tough discipline, there was the poor food, supplemented only by such fish as could be caught and fresh fruit bought at stopping places, while living space was confined to cramped, murky quarters in the fo'c'sle. Yet in song and story sperm-whaling has become a romance, that is an adventure and excitement. The hard, dangerous, yet everyday, work of the whale-crews would now be thought of as adventure worthy of the publicity given to the climbing of mountains or the sailing of small boats by people whose thirst for physical excitement and achievement cannot be satisfied by the tameness of modern life.

Out of the routine of trimming sails and working up whales there stand some episodes that show up sperm-whaling as an exciting and adventurous occupation. Such stories fire the imagination; they may cause a sense of loss that such things no longer happen and that 'running away to sea' is no longer worth the dreams of an adventurous boy. Yet when they happened they could not have been fun or exciting, merely terrifying and agonizing. It is a strange quirk of human nature that stories of boldly facing up to danger that lead men to join risky operations, whether military, professional or exploratory, usually concern just those incidents which are better avoided by anyone who values his life.

One such story is that of the disaster that befell the American North Pacific whaling fleet when beset by ice, and is described in the next chapter. The fate of the Nantucket ship *Essex* is yet more incredible and although it was a disaster on a smaller scale, the suffering was infinitely greater. In November 1820 the *Essex* was working near the equator, midway between the Marquesas and the Galapagos. While chasing sperm whales the boat belonging to Owen Chase, the mate, was struck and had to set back to the ship. Not long after, Chase saw a large sperm whale near by. It immediately turned towards the ship and rammed it at full speed. The shock jarred the ship, leaving it quivering and leaking badly, but as soon as the pumps had been rigged, the whale struck again and stove in the bows.

This was not the first time that a ship had been struck by a sperm whale. In this case the first collision was probably accidental while the second may have been inspired by rage. The question was academic to the men on the *Essex*, as she rapidly settled. Grabbing some navigational equipment, they jumped into Owen Chase's damaged whale boat and drew away to await the return of the other two boats. The captain was the first to draw near. The poor man was shattered by the sudden and apparently inexplicable wreck of his ship. 'My God, Mr Chase, what is the matter?' Chase answered, 'We have been stove by a whale' – a succinct dialogue, as memorable as 'Dr Livingstone, I presume.'

The *Essex* had not completely disappeared and the men were able to retrieve a small quantity of food and gear before they set sail for the American mainland, so avoiding the Marquesas, which they believed to be inhabited by cannibals, and the Sandwich Islands where a hurricane season was thought to be in progress. Nearly four weeks later they sighted land, the small and almost barren Henderson's Island. After a week they set off again, leaving three men there, and their suffering took a new and grisly turn. Racked by hunger and thirst, as well as by their desperate situation, three of the crew died. But, in doing so, they saved their companions, who forced themselves to eat their flesh.

Chase's boat became separated from the others and was picked up by a ship after covering 6,000 kilometres. The other two boats had a worse fate. One disappeared without trace and in the captain's boat the survivors ran out of food. There was only one thing to do. Lots were cast, and Owen Coffin, the captain's nephew, lost. He was killed and eaten. Three weeks later, three months after leaving the *Essex*, the survivors were picked up. Of the nine men that survived the wreck of the *Essex*, all went back to sea and all eventually gained command of ships.

The story of the *Essex* must be one of the grimmest episodes in the history of whaling, but lesser disasters were frequent as the men battled with their giant quarry. Strokes from the lashing flukes caused death or ghastly wounds and the harpoon line accounted for injuries ranging from burns to death by drowning as it was swept out of the boat by the whale. Scammon tells of an officer, nicknamed 'Jabe', who was entangled in a line and only saved by the harpoon drawing out, and Svend Føyn later suffered a similar accident. Scammon also records the accidents that befell the crew of one ship in the course of one day's whaling. The whale struck one boat, breaking the leg of one man and the arm of another, together with minor injuries to others. A second boat, coming to help, was also struck causing injuries to many of the crew. All were eventually rescued but half the ship's company had been injured and most of the rest badly frightened. Two boats were launched a few days later but the crews jumped overboard as soon as they neared a whale. However, even this panic-stricken action could have its amusing side, as when a notorious braggart leaped headlong over the side of his boat and landed on the whale's back. The whale slowly submerged leaving the man floundering.

The decline of the sperm-whalers was gradual and almost painless. From its discovery in 1858, the use of mineral oil developed gradually so that the demand for sperm-oil fell only slowly. Whalebone from bowheads, humpbacks and gray whales was still in demand and made whaling voyages profitable. So there was no sudden laying up of ships and no unemployment.

Whale-ships continued to sail out of New England and Pacific ports, but in ever decreasing numbers, until World War One when U-boat warfare created a shortage of oils and fats and demand for whale-oil rose again. In 1918 there was an attempt in the United States to introduce whalemeat for human consumption. The meat was cut up, cooled, soaked in brine to remove blood and the strong taste, then tinned. The experiment was not a success and the old-time Yankee sperm-whalers eventually died out, the end coming in 1925 when the *John R. Manta* and the *Margarett* returned to New Bedford from their last cruises.

The Americans had, however, left a legacy in the form of open-boat whaling in other parts of the world.

In the early part of the nineteenth century there had been a considerable sperm-whale fishery around the coasts of Australia and New Zealand. Later the colonists there took up the chase and developed a flourishing industry for both sperm whales and humpbacks. This continued as a relic industry until 1932 at Twofold Bay in New South Wales, by which time modern whaling with steam catchers had commenced. At the turn of the century one shore station in New Zealand employed strong nets for catching humpbacks. The whales became entangled as they swam close inshore and were lanced from boats.

Open-boat whaling using equipment identical to that used by American sperm-whalers had survived in two parts of the North Atlantic: in the West Indies and the Azores. The American whale-ships called at both groups of islands to pick up native boatmen as crew, and they developed the local whaling industries on their return.

In the West Indies, whaling is still carried on at St Vincent, St Lucia and Dominica. The catch once included humpbacks and sperm whales but now it is the smaller cetaceans, such as pilot whales, which are the main catch. Despite the introduction of outboard motors and shotguns to hurl the harpoon 50 metres, much farther than is possible by throwing, this little industry which used to account for several hundred whales and porpoises in a year, is probably doomed to wither as the tourist trade blossoms and provides easier ways of making a living. As a comment on the role of romance and excitement in whaling, one West Indian skipper gave it as his ambition to leave his boat and get a job in North America as a petrol station attendant.

The sperm-whaling industry based in the Azores is better known and is still flourishing with the addition of motor boats to tow the whale-boats close to the whale, and to tow the carcase back, and radio sets for the look-outs to guide the whalers to their target. A detailed study of the techniques still in use has been made by Robert Clarke, who found that few innovations have been made. As already mentioned the boat-header and boatsteerer do not change ends, the boat is longer than the American original and carries one more oarsman, otherwise the whalers of the Azores and West Indies are a living relic of bygone days. Until recently most of whales caught around the Azores were still tried-out in iron pots on the shore, as they had been in seventeenth-century New England and Spitzbergen.

Bowheads and Gray Whales

As the number of sperm whales caught began to drop during the nineteenth century, more whalers turned to the Arctic regions of the Atlantic, where European whalers had been fishing sporadically since the seventeenth century for Greenland right whales or bowheads. Some time later, the American Pacific fleet entered the Sea of Okhotsk, the Bering Sea and finally penetrated the Bering Straits into the Arctic Ocean. The right whales were not such dangerous quarry as sperm whales, but working in northern seas brought the constant danger of being trapped by ice. Many ships were lost, sometimes whole fleets at a time, but their crews often escaped to other ships or reached land where they were sheltered by Eskimos.

Unlike the sperm-whalers, the right whale hunters were limited to short summer cruises, when the seas were relatively free from ice. British whalers left their home ports, such as Hull, Whitby and Dundee, in early March and called at Lerwick in the Shetland Islands to replenish their stores and sign on local men to complete their crews. As soon as the ship was sailing steadily northwards the boats' crews were chosen in a way that ensured a fair distribution and no favour. The crew lined up in rows and the harpooners gave their pocket knives to a boy who had never been to sea before. He laid one knife, not knowing to whom it belonged, in front of each row of men and they became the crew of the knife's owner. The crews then set to preparing the whaling gear, sharpening harpoons and lances and coiling the whale lines so that they were free of kinks.

During this period, at least, the whale ship's crew were full of hope for success in what was one of the most speculative of occupations during this period. A successful season would result in a full pocket on the return home, but it was not unknown for a ship to come home empty. This meant poverty for the crew because they were paid starvation wages, any profit coming in the form of bonuses or bounties. At one time harpooners received no pay except bounties, but in 1850 they received thirty shillings per month, which was supplemented by bounties at the rate of twenty shillings per ton of whalebone, eight shillings per ton of oil and eight shillings for each whale harpooned. Mates were paid fifty-five shillings a month with proportionately larger bounties, but, as the crew had to buy their own tea, coffee, tobacco and other luxuries, they could come home from an unsuccessful cruise actually in debt. Those with families had to join coal ships for the winter, a blow to their pride as well as the loss of a well-earned rest.

When whales were scarce the whalers attempted to cut their losses by hunting seals, walruses and polar bears, particularly when heavy ice made whale-hunting impossible. Polar bears were also an additional prize when they gathered to feed off a whale carcase. They were usually shot and skinned – one ship killed forty-five out of sixty bears they found at a carcase. Young bears were sometimes caught alive for zoos. A fine bear was worth £35, a good price in those days, but even a young polar bear needs to be treated with care. The best way of catching a bear was to throw a lasso over its neck as it was swimming and pull in the slack rope until the bear was hard against the side of the boat. There is a story of one harpooner who neglected to secure the rope properly. The bear jumped aboard and the frightened crew scurried aft, leaving their weapons in the bows, but luckily the bear was just as scared and jumped out again.

A far less hazardous pastime was the killing of seals. Harp seals bear their young in March and the whaling-ships called at the breeding grounds on the ice on their way north. Both adults and pups were killed by clubbing or rifle fire, and their bodies carried on board for the skins to be removed and salted, while the blubber was packed in barrels. If a ship found a large concentration of pups its crew could dispose of 2,500 in a day, hard work when the pups were in peak condition, weighing about 35 kilograms, and dangerous, too, if the ice were broken and a swell was running.

Even such a vast slaughter of seals was no more than a

sideline to the serious business of whale-catching. The boom in right-whaling in Arctic waters started in the second decade of the nineteenth century and between 1814 and 1817 there were nearly one hundred and fifty British ships working there each year. Up to this time most whalers had worked in the Greenland Sea, to the north of Iceland, with only a few sailing round the southern tip of Greenland into the Davis Strait. These grounds were poor, but in 1817 two ships got past Disko Island into Baffin Bay (see Figure 16, p. 148) where they found whales to be plentiful. In the following years the Greenland Sea was virtually abandoned by all except Scandinavian sealers in favour of the rich hunting grounds on the east and west coasts of Baffin Bay. The situation was summed up by the expression: *Dusky dipping, whale fish skipping* (Dusky = Disko; dipping = on the horizon).

The ships that sailed into the ice-infested waters west of Greenland had of necessity to be more strongly built than the ships engaged in sperm-whaling, and no right-whaler suffered the fate of the *Essex*. However, their equipment was much the same, except that the lookout nestled in a barrel-like crow's nest rather than hanging onto an iron loop, and the blubber was stored in iron tanks without being tried-out. An important development in the early nineteenth century was the introduction of various types of harpoon guns. These were small compared with Svend Føyn's modern guns and were often hand-held.

Several attempts had been made to find ways of propelling a harpoon farther than could be effected by a man's strength. Harpoon guns were first tried out in the eighteenth century but they were not adopted because of reluctance to give up old, well-tried methods; a reluctance reinforced by accidents and the loss of whales through inexperience. Nevertheless, in 1772 the Society of Arts tried to popularize an improved version of its own gun by offering £1 for the best account of taking whales with it. This gun could hurl a harpoon forty metres, a great improvement over the range of the hand harpoon. Like modern harpoons, this harpoon had a slip-ring on the shaft that slid back to the butt and allowed the whaleline to steady the harpoon's flight.

By the 1850s most British ships carried harpoon guns that were mounted on swivels in the boats' bows. The Americans took longer to adopt them but during the second half of the century both nationalities hunted right whales with a strange assortment of firearms. The basic harpoon gun was Greener's gun. It had a three-foot barrel, a bore of 4 centimetres and fired a 1·4-metre harpoon about 75 metres with reasonable accuracy. After 1858 a new device began to supersede the hand lance. This was the bomb-lance which was fired either from the same Greener's gun as the harpoon or from a separate firearm. The bomb-lance consisted of a metal tube about 53 centimetres long with a sharp tip. As it left the gun elastic fins unrolled from the tube to steady its flight, and a fuse was lit as the gun went off to detonate the powder charge after the bomb-lance had penetrated the whale.

With these two weapons whales could be killed without the boat having to come within twenty-five metres and the dangers of the enterprise were considerably reduced. A third weapon was a combined hand harpoon and bomb-lance that dispensed with the dangers of using firearms in a small boat. It was an

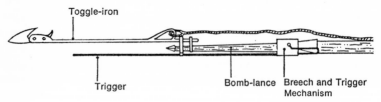

Figure 15 Pierce's harpoon-bomb-lance-gun (modified from Scammon).

ingenious mechanism known by the cumbersome name of Pierce's harpoon-bomb-lance-gun. To the tip of a conventional harpoon shaft was attached the lock and 30-centimetre barrel of the gun. A toggle-iron harpoon was clamped to the muzzle end of the barrel which was loaded with a 40-centimetre bomb-lance. The contrivance was darted at the whale by hand so that the harpoon made fast. As it entered the whale the trigger rod was pushed back tripping the firing mechanism and shooting the bomb-lance deep into the whale's body where it was detonated by a time fuse. The harpoon and its attached line came free so that the shaft and the precious gun could be hauled back to the boat on a thin line, while the harpoon was still fast.

Even with the help of explosives right whales might take over twenty hours to kill, leaving the boat crew tired and frozen from the effort. Perhaps this was the least of their worries, because the Davis Strait and Baffin Bay were notorious for their ice. As well as icebergs there was heavy pack ice, thick floes that drifted down from the Arctic Ocean. If the whalers were lucky the ice broke up early in the spring and drifted southwards leaving open water. If not, they had to weave their way up leads of open water that might close as any moment, trapping the ship and perhaps crushing it. In this part of the world gales suddenly spring up, forcing the floes together and riding over each other, while icebergs drive through the pack crushing everything in their way. Even in a flat calm, when the surface of the sea is like a mirror, the pack ice may eerily creep forward, driven by currents or distant gales.

Against these overwhelming forces the whalers had to rely chiefly on luck, but experience and expertise could help to alleviate the dangers. As far as was possible, the ships hugged the coastline. For one thing this was the place to find the whales, and if the ships could keep close inshore they avoided the largest floes and icebergs which grounded on the bottom offshore. The disadvantages of this practice were running onto rocks in the uncharted waters and the danger of onshore winds driving them aground.

If a ship was caught by pack ice in the open sea, one chance of avoiding being crushed was to saw docks in a large floe. Using 5-metre saws mounted on rockers and operated by sixteen men, a large chunk of ice could be cut out and floated away to form a deep slot. The ship was worked into the slot and moored with sea anchors. Here it was safe from the pressure of the ice outside, unless the floe forming the dock split up. If the floes did grip the ship, the crew's salvation lay in the ice sliding under the keel to lift up the ship because if the ship was nipped on the waterline the floes might splinter her timbers. Pressure from ice was alleviated by use of saws and explosive charges and the ship could sometimes be freed by breaking the ice with artificial waves. A stout rope was run

from the masthead to the ice and the crew hauled rhythmically, rolling the ship, to shatter the ice around the hull.

Whaling-ships were all too often caught by ice near the end
of the season. Unless a gale broke the ice and blew it away they
were then in danger of being trapped for the winter. The crews
had to prepare for the worst by moving stores onto land, if
there was any nearby, and by hunting for seals or fishing.
Sometimes there would be other ships nearby that were clear
of ice and half the men of the trapped ship would attempt to
reach them by dragging their boats over the ice to open water.
This hazardous undertaking was necessary because the ships
did not carry enough supplies to feed the whole crew throughout an Arctic winter. This lack of foresight, or rather mean-
ness, on the part of the ships' owners was to have disastrous
consequences.

It had become the habit of the whalers to leave the relatively
open waters of the west coast of Greenland and sail across
Baffin Bay to Baffin Island where they would go 'rock nosing' –
threading their way through the deep bays where whales
abounded. There was a particular danger of being trapped by
ice floes piling across the entrance of the bay, and disaster came
in 1830 when severe weather destroyed nineteen out of the
ninety-one British ships that entered the Davis Strait. Hardly a
whale was caught and some whaling companies were put out
of business. The remainder continued as before and in 1835 six
more ships were lost and a further eleven were stuck in the ice
for the winter. Although five were freed in the spring their
crew suffered horribly. Weakened by shortage of food, they
succumbed easily to frostbite and scurvy. Out of six hundred
men in the fleet, one fifth perished.

The incredible sequel to the disaster of 1835 is that the ship
owners completely ignored its lessons and sent their ships back
to the Davis Strait in 1836 still without adequate provisions for
an enforced stay. Once again the ice closed in and six ships
were trapped for the winter with all the ensuing suffering. It
was only then that remedies were debated. Some ships began to
carry the new invention of tinned food, and the idea of wintering at a permanent base to cut out the dangerous journeys in
and out of the Davis Strait was considered. One of the chief
protagonists of wintering in the Arctic was Captain (later Sir)

James Clark Ross, the famous explorer, who had been sent to the whalers' aid in HMS *Cove* in 1835.

The idea of spending winter at land stations was nearly as old as Arctic whaling itself. The first attempt was made by the English during the days of whaling at Spitzbergen. Volunteers to spend a winter at the whaling station at Spitzbergen were sought but none came forward, so a handful of condemned criminals were offered a free pardon if they would spend the winter there. Overjoyed, they were conveyed north but after one look at the grim, desolate scenery, they expressed preference for a quick death. They were, in fact, pardoned, but their misgivings about Spitzbergen were justified because Dutch parties left for the winter were wiped out by scurvy. That Europeans could survive an Arctic winter was proved by accident when a group of English whalers was marooned at a shore station. They survived a terrible winter by hunting and chewing the fritters left over from the summer's blubber boiling.

Ross's suggestions for a permanent base were taken up by William Penny, who later became famous for his expeditions in search of Sir John Franklin after he had failed to return from an attempt to find the North-west Passage. It was through Penny that whalers penetrated Cumberland Sound where a flourishing fishery later developed. Increasing numbers of whalers, particularly Americans, took to wintering in ships or on the shore. They went out on sorties from their bases in early spring to hunt whales amongst the floes, dragging the blubber and whalebone back over the ice. The Cumberland Sound fishery flourished until the 1860s when the Americans opened up Hudson's Bay, but shore stations continued there until the 1930s.

The whalers could heave a sigh of relief as they cleared the last of the ice at the end of the season. All was set for a clear run home unless they ran into trouble with bad weather or hostile ships. During the Napoleonic wars French corvettes disguised as whale-ships captured and burnt some British ships, but one captain saw through their deception. Seeing the corvette from a distance he realized that the impostor's whaling gear was mounted on the starboard rather than the port side, as was usual, and made his escape into some pack ice.

Even on their arrival home the whale crews were not safe and were subjected to a practice that they bitterly resented. This was the press-gang operated by a navy desperately short of seamen. The higher grades of whalemen, the harpooners and boat-steerers, were exempt from the press provided they could get tickets from the Customs officers. To reach the officers and claim their tickets the men had to resort to subterfuge, dressing as women, being carried in barrels, or arming themselves with harpoons and lances and marching to the Customs in force.

William Scoresby once saved his crew when a revenue cutter bore down on them by opening a tap in the hull that was normally used for filling ballast casks. The ship began to fill with water and the men were set to work the pumps. When the revenue officer came on board Scoresby pointed out that if any of his crew were taken the ship would sink. The officer was not easily fooled. He ordered pumping to cease and checked for himself that the water level started to rise. Satisfied that there really was a leak he returned to his ship. Scoresby turned off the tap, his men pumped the hold dry and the ship reached home safely.

The British Arctic whale fishery did not decline in the same manner as that of the American sperm-whalers. Although disasters such as those of 1835 and 1836 set the industry back it seemed to be more adaptable than the larger New England industry. The British whalers were quicker to use firearms and quickly saw the advantages of steam. Tugboats had been used regularly to tow the whale-ships out of harbour but in 1852 Sir Edward Belcher's expedition in search of Franklin used their tug to tow a Dundee whale-ship to the coast of Baffin Island. The Americans did not use tugs in the Arctic until 1882 although Thomas Williams shipped a small steamboat on the deck of his whaler in 1878, using it to chase whales among the floes.

William Penny had plans to convert a whale-ship to steam in 1853 and in 1858 an engine was installed in a Dundee ship. Steam power was only used as an accessory to sail but it took much of the misery out of Arctic navigation. No longer did becalmed ships have to wait helplessly as ice drifted towards them, nor did they have to claw away from rocky shores in the face of the wind. Before the introduction of steam the only way to move a becalmed ship was for the crew to tow it with the boats or 'track' it by dragging it on foot along the edges of floes, perhaps for scores of miles. Now they could admire the view from the deck as they steamed through the ice. The ship could also steam into the wind to go to the assistance of its boats as they laboriously towed their catch. The main danger was that the screw might be broken if it hit a floe.

Another experiment at the same time failed dismally. Iron steamers were built at Hull and Peterhead. Six set out in 1859, two sank after their first contact with ice and the remainder were distinctly unsuccessful. Not for another seventy years could iron-hulled ships compete with tough, resilient wooden hulls for safety in ice.

About the same time as the Americans were turning their attention to right whales in the seas around Greenland, their Pacific fleets were augmenting their catch of sperm whales with Greenland right whales or bowheads. Previously they had been taken in several parts of the Pacific but in 1835 they were discovered in the Kodiak ground off Alaska and in 1843 they were found off Kamchatka. In the following years they were pursued in the Okhotsk Sea and in 1848 Captain Royce of the *Superior* passed through the Bering Straits into the Arctic Ocean.

The onslaught on the bowheads became the final upsurge of American whaling. Based mainly on San Francisco and Honolulu the whalers cruised both the North and the South Pacific. At the start of the voyage they sailed south on the 'between season cruise', hunting sperm whales and breaking in the crews for the bowhead fishing that started as the ice broke up. There was an appalling waste of a rich natural resource in bowhead whaling. Before the stocks became diminished the whalers sometimes took the whalebone only. They reckoned that it was quicker and more profitable to kill another whale than to go to the trouble of cutting-in and trying-out the first.

The happy state of the bowhead fishery lasted until 1871, when it was dealt a severe blow similar to the disaster that befell the British fleet in the 1830s. Ships had been lost in the ice every year but in 1871 only seven whale-ships survived out of the fleet of about thirty-five that had sailed north.

As was their habit the fleet had followed the bowheads on

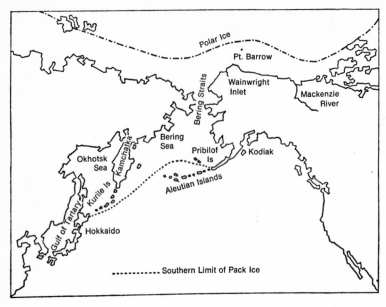

their northward migration from the vicinity of Japan into the
Bering Sea and then up to the Arctic Ocean. This year they
found heavy ice in the Bering Sea and one ship was crushed
there. The Bering Straits were finally penetrated in June, but
there was so much ice that whaling was barely possible and the
whalers filled in time by hunting walruses. Only in the final
days of July did the ice clear sufficiently for whaling to start in

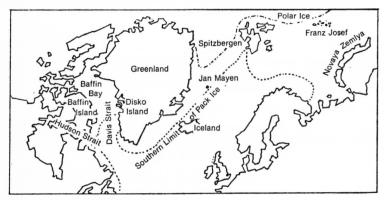

Figure 16 **The Arctic whaling grounds.**

earnest. The fleet worked its way up the coast of Alaska making for Point Barrow on the northernmost tip of Alaska. But on August 29th a strong wind sprung from the south-west and the ice began to close in, forcing the ships towards the shore and trapping them between two headlands near Wainright Inlet. Thirty-four ships were caught there while a further seven lay at the edge of the pack ice at Icy Cape, some 110 kilometres to the south.

At first the situation did not seem too desperate as the thick ice floes around the ships were resting on the seabed and it only needed a change of wind to blow them away. But the change never came and tremendous pressure built up in the pack ice so that it was gradually forced over the seabed and onto the shore. The ships could not escape and on September 2nd the first was crushed. Within a week two more were wrecked. In one case the floes suddenly parted and the crushed husk of the ship dropped between them, giving the crew barely time to jump onto the ice.

It was now obvious that there was little chance of the fleet getting clear and a boat was dispatched to Icy Cape to ask the ships there to stand by. On the 14th about 1,200 men, together with the families of several of the captains, set out in the boats, abandoning their ships in order to run for those waiting outside the pack. They made the journey in two days, battling through snowstorms and freshly forming ice, but they reached the safety of the waiting ships and all eventually arrived in Honolulu.

The sequel to this disaster that threw several ship-owners out of business was galling in the extreme. Less than two weeks after the ships had been abandoned the long-hoped for north-easterly gale sprung up and cleared the pack ice. But it was too late; only one ship was saved when the whalers returned the following year. The others had sunk, been carried away in the ice or had been burnt by Eskimos.

While hunting bowheads in the northern seas, the whalers sometimes took other species as they presented themselves, such as humpbacks and gray whales. These two also became the object of an intense, but short-lived, fishery that flourished along the coast of Upper and Lower California. It was in 1846 that whalers first came to hunt along these arid shores in the late winter before sailing up to the Arctic. By 1848, fifty ships were taking part in what became known as 'bay-whaling' or 'kelp-whaling', whose season ran from December to February as the whales migrated close to the land.

On arrival at the estuaries and lagoons of California the whale-ships were securely moored, the sails and sailing gear removed and the cutting stage erected. In later years ships were dispensed with, shore stations set up and the whales were cut-in and tried-out on the beach after the manner of the seventeenth-century New Englanders and the Basques before them.

When sufficient numbers of gray whales had congregated in the lagoons the boats were launched in their pursuit. This was the most dangerous whaling of all. The shallow lagoons gave neither boats nor whales much room to manœuvre and the gray whales were aggressive, earning themselves the name of devil-fish. More powerful than right whales and faster than sperm whales, harpooned gray whales careered about the lagoons capsizing boats and entangling whale-lines. The casualties to boats and men were high as the whales would attack without provocation.

Greener's guns were essential to harpoon these swift creatures and the whalers preferred to harpoon those that were accompanied by calves. They had, of necessity, to swim slowly so it was easier to close with them both for harpooning and delivering the *coup de grâce* with a bomb-lance. Another tactic was for the whalers to lie in wait with their boats in the beds of kelp and shoot the whales as they passed.

In a year or so the whales became wary of the waiting whale-boats and these were substituted by small boats carrying one oarsman and a gunner. This ruse lasted several seasons after which it was impossible to approach the whale without alarming it and it had to be chased until a bomb could be fired into it. When it had slowed down, a harpoon was struck into its body so that when it died and sank the position could be marked with a buoy. About a day later the carcase would rise to the surface and be towed in for flensing. An even more callous method was the harpooning of a calf and dragging it ashore so that the parent could be shot from the beach as it attempted to succour its offspring. A final method was to follow and overtake the migrating whales in boats under sail, known as 'sailing them down'.

Despite the dangers that killed or crippled many a whaler, bay-whaling was extremely popular and was prosecuted with incredible zeal. Ships were lightened and dragged over shoals into the lagoons, where they could easily be endangered by sudden gales and the harpooners did not stop at striking 'devil-fish'. They also attacked the yet larger and faster blue whales and fin whales although these rorquals were usually left alone because of the difficulty of catching them and the poor quality of their oil and whalebone.

In 1851 Scammon estimated that a thousand or more gray whales passed down the coast each day. About twenty years later this number had been reduced to forty and early in the twentieth century the Californian gray whale was thought to be extinct. In fact, it had survived in very small numbers and, under strict protection, it has recovered.

13 | The Final Phase

THE quest for new sources of whales became urgent at the end of the nineteenth century. The Arctic grounds were almost spent and the Norwegians and Americans were beginning to hunt rorquals in the North Atlantic, the only untapped reserve of large whales remaining in the northern hemisphere. In the southern hemisphere there still remained the largest concentration of whales in the world. In 1892 four Scottish whale-ships left Dundee for the Southern Ocean. Their commission was based on a report by Sir James Clark Ross who had sailed deep into the Weddell Sea in 1844. He wrote:

> We observed a very great number of the largest-sized black (right) whales, so tame that they allowed the ship sometimes almost to touch them before they would get out of the way; so that any number of ships might procure a cargo of oil in a short time. Thus . . . we had discovered . . . a valuable whale-fishery well worth the attention of our enterprising merchants!

Ross was one of the most respected polar explorers so the Dundee whalers had every right to be optimistic. But the expedition was a failure; they had been forestalled by both British and American whalers who had often turned from sperm-whaling to hunt right whales in polar waters, or to catch them as they migrated into warmer waters. The Scotsmen drew a complete blank and, in desperation, one harpooner struck at a blue whale. The line raced out and that from another boat had to be bent on. This was insufficient and a third boat was brought in. The whale was now towing six lines and three boats and the men managed to get a line to the parent ship, which was added to the procession moving over the sea. Fourteen hours later, the whale's rush had still not abated, so the ship's engines were put astern, and the line snapped.

There must have been considerable gloom on board the

four ships as they made their way back up the Atlantic. There were no longer sufficient right whales to support the industry but the expedition had unwittingly missed the chance of establishing a considerable fishery for humpbacks which existed in large numbers around South Georgia, a large island on the fringes of the Southern Ocean. Despite the failure with the blue whale, ways had now been found to hunt the faster rorquals and a rorqual fishery was already in existence in the North Atlantic, thanks to the inventiveness and persistence of one man, the Norwegian Svend Føyn, whose work eventually paved the way to the establishment of whaling in the Antarctic.

A sealer by trade, Føyn had long been interested in whaling and had reached the conclusion that the industry could only survive if some way could be found of hunting the rorquals. Some had been killed with bomb-lances and rockets, but handling large, non-buoyant carcases was still a problem. Føyn spent several years experimenting and finally brought into being the technique that revolutionized whale-hunting.

Svend Føyn's basic invention was a powerful harpoon gun, far superior to Greener's gun and its contemporaries which were little more than hand-guns mounted in a standard whale-boat. Føyn's gun was a heavy cannon mounted in the bows of a small steam vessel. It fired a large harpoon with an explosive head that severely wounded or killed the whale, and trailed a 13-centimetre line so that the dead whale could be winched to the surface and filled with compressed air to prevent it from sinking.

Føyn's ship, the *Spes et Fides*, had its first successful cruise in 1868 when he caught thirty whales in Varanger Fjord. At last it was possible to make fast to the largest whales, kill them, prevent them from sinking, then tow them home. And it was all done in comparative safety. One hundred years later harpoon guns and whale-catchers are still recognizable as having evolved from Svend Føyn's prototype, although modern catchers are about five times the gross weight of the *Spes et Fides* and have a maximum speed of eighteen knots.

The original Føyn harpoon guns were muzzle-loaders but nowadays breech-loaders are used, employing 400 grams of smokeless powder to propel a 70-kilogram, 1·8-metre harpoon. When ready for firing the harpoon has a grenade containing

170 grams of powder screwed to the tip. A time fuse is set to detonate the grenade after the harpoon has entered the whale, so crippling or, with luck, killing it. An innovation is a saucer-shaped rather than pointed tip to the harpoon head to prevent ricochets and make the harpoon turn downwards if it strikes a glancing blow. Behind the grenade are four barbed flukes that pivot on hinges and fly out after the harpoon is embedded in the whale. Until then they are tied against the shaft with cord, and the whole harpoon is held in the barrel of the gun with more cord. The front section of the shaft, which bears the flukes and grenade, pivots on the main length. While the flukes are tied in place they hold the two sections rigid but after they have flown out the main part of the shaft is free to fold along the whale's back, so reducing the drag and preventing the harpoon head from being pulled out (see Figure 17).

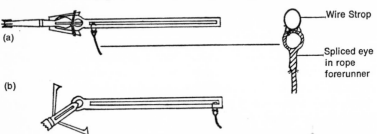

Figure 17 Modern harpoon (a) before firing and (b) after striking the whale, when the grenade has exploded and the flukes have spread.

The 7·5-centimetre diameter shaft has a slot running most of its length. The slot takes a wire loop to which the whale-line is attached. When the gun is fired, the loop slides to the base of the harpoon shaft and the line follows cleanly, steadying the flight of the harpoon instead of dragging it down.

The gun is mounted on a platform over the bows of the whale-catcher. There has been a trend to raise the height of the bows almost to a level with the bridge, which is connected to the platform by a catwalk so that the skipper, who is also gunner, can guide the catcher up to the whale, then race down to the gun at the last minute.

The rope attached to the harpoon consists first of a 130-metre forerunner, formerly of hemp, now of nylon. To this is attached

200-metre lengths of manilla. When the whale is harpooned the rope is hauled in by a heavy winch mounted just forward of the deckhouse. But even 23 centimetres manilla cannot stand the strain of being stretched between a desperate, wounded whale and a whale-catcher bouncing over the waves. The whale has, therefore, to be played as a salmon is played on the finest tackle. Line is let out or taken in as the pull on it varies and, to prevent sudden tugs snapping the line, it is passed through the whalers' equivalent of flexible fishing rod. The line travels from the winch to a sheave half-way up the mast, and down to the bows (see Figure 18). The sheave is attached to a rope that runs to the masthead and down to a series of accumulator springs in the hold. As tension in the whale-line increases the sheave is pulled down, the springs are stretched and the strain on the whale-line decreases. So movements of whale and catcher are continually being buffered by play in the accumulator springs.

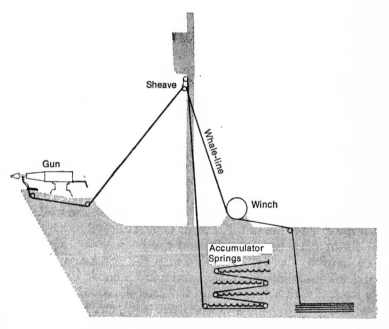

Figure 18 The spring mechanism of a whale-catcher that reduces the tension and cushions shocks in the whale-line.

The range of a modern harpoon gun is 90 metres at the outside and gunners prefer to shoot when the whale is not more than 50 metres away. To get within range the catcher has to be brought up to the whale, not an easy job even with the latest in fast catchers. Until 1937 all catchers were steam-powered, a silent form of propulsion that allowed the whalers to stalk their quarry by what the Norwegians call *luse jag*. In this method whales are sighted from the crow's nest and a watch is kept to ascertain their course and the frequency with which they blow. The catcher closes with them at full speed then slows down and is manœuvred into position so that it will be just behind the chosen whale as it blows. The gunner then rushes down to his gun and gives final instructions by hand signals. As the whale's back humps out of the water, he sights along the aiming rod above the gun barrel and fires.

When noisy but more powerful diesel engines were introduced it was no longer possible to creep up on a whale. Instead, the whales are chased, a technique called *prøyser jag*. As they become tired they slow down and have to blow more frequently. If chased hard they have to surface every two or three minutes and in a quarter to half an hour they will have slowed sufficiently for the catcher to close in. Since World War Two echolocating sonar equipment has been used to track whales underwater and, as the high frequency pulses emitted by sonar frightens whales, it has been used to assist in the technique of *prøyser jag*.

If the whale is not killed outright it must be carefully played by the gunner passing instructions to the helmsman and the engineer who controls the winch, until further harpoons can be shot into it. As soon as there is no life left, it is brought alongside and secured by a chain passed around the stock, the narrow part of the tail. A hollow lance attached to an airline is thrust deep into its belly and the body cavity is inflated. To improve the catcher's efficiency the carcase is released and left to drift while more whales are hunted. Each whale is marked with a flag bearing the catcher's number, a radar reflector and a radio beacon. Eventually the whale is collected by the catcher and towed home with the rest of its catch. When whales were abundant it might stagger in with two carcases on each side, and special buoy-boats have been employed in towing, to relieve the catchers of even this chore.

When Svend Føyn first started operations he hunted only blue whales. As the largest species of whale it gave the greatest yield of oil for a given effort. His success stimulated the formation of other companies who turned their attention to other species of rorquals. Catching operations using Føyn harpoon guns and based on simple shore factories spread around the North Atlantic, from Spitzbergen to Ireland, into the North Pacific and later to all whaling grounds. The moment was now ripe for the rich Antarctic grounds to be opened. The right whales reported by Sir James Clark Ross were now rare but the Southern Ocean was still the home of vast populations of rorquals, particularly humpbacks, blue whales and fin whales.

The first man to exploit this potential was the Norwegian Carl Anton Larsen. His first visit to the Antarctic was in search of seals but he saw the possibility of hunting rorquals there. In 1902 he returned to these waters as the captain of the *Antarctic*, the ship carrying Nordenskjöld's Swedish South Polar Expedition. The *Antarctic* was lost and after many adventures the crew and explorers were rescued by an Argentinian gunboat and taken back to Buenos Aires. Here Larsen put forward his plan to set up a whaling factory to process whales caught in the Antarctic. He secured the necessary financial backing and in 1904 three ships of the *Compania Argentina de Pesca* arrived in the cove of Grytviken, at the head of Cumberland Bay in South Georgia.

When Larsen's expedition arrived at South Georgia whales abounded and his single whale-catcher found sufficient whales, mainly humpbacks, without having to leave Cumberland Bay. As soon as one was caught it was towed back to Grytviken where a factory had been built from materials brought by the other two ships. The whaling factory at Grytviken continued in use with very little change from 1904 to 1963 and its layout and operations were similar to those of shore factories throughout the world. Like the old shore factories of Spitzbergen, a modern whale factory is a production line for dismembering and processing whale carcases, but on a much larger scale than those at Smeerenburg. Motor winches and steam saws serve to make easy the work that had once to be done by man-power and hand tools, and at Grytviken a steady procession of whale carcases passed through the factory. On an exceptional day thirty fin whales could disappear into the boilers.

The activities of the factory are centred on the plan, a large area just above the shoreline covered with baulks of timber to give a solid working surface. The whale is winched tail-first up a slipway and on to the plan where, almost before it has come to a standstill, it is attacked by a gang of men known in Norwegian as *flensers*. They are armed with long-handled razor-sharp knives with which they slice great slits down the length of the whale. Wires are attached to the blubber and wound in by the winch so that strips of blubber are torn off the underlying flesh, with the assistance of the flensers' knives, and the whale is peeled like a gigantic banana. The remainder of the carcase, known as the *skrot*, is turned over and pulled to one side of the plan leaving room for another whale to be drawn up the slipway. While the flensers attack the second whale, the skrot of the first is skilfully trimmed of its meat and the skeleton is dismembered by the meat-cutting men or *lemmers*.

The blubber, meat and bones are processed separately, each receiving treatment that depends largely on the state of the market for different products. In the early days of Antarctic whaling, the whales were so abundant that the carcases were merely stripped of their blubber and discarded. This was an incredible waste of raw material and was soon stopped by economic factors and by law, the meat and bones then being processed for oil and the residue used as meatmeal and bone-meal. After the war years there was a market for whalemeat for human consumption in western countries but it never became popular and it is now fed to animals. In Japan, how-ever, whalemeat is used in several forms and it is shipped back to Japan in refrigerator ships.

The economic success of the modern phase of whaling is due to one invention. In the early twentieth century the process of hydrogenation was discovered and it became possible to turn a liquid oil into a solid and odourless fat. Immediately a new market was opened for whale-oil, whose sales had been decreas-ing since the introduction of petroleum oil. The oil of whale-bone whales is a glyceride made of fatty acids and glycerol, like the oil from most animal fats, but unlike the waxy oils of sperm whales. In hydrogenation the oil is 'hardened' or 'saturated' by adding extra hydrogen atoms to each molecule of glyceride to turn it into a solid fat. In this form whale-oil can be used in the manufacture of soap and margarine. Glycerine is a by-product of soap manufacture which has many industrial uses, and other applications of whale-oil products include the manufacture of varnishes, printing ink, explosives and cosmetics.

Whale-oil has almost always been the principal product of whaling, and at Grytviken and similar stations the whole whale carcase was boiled down for oil. As soon as the sheets of blubber have been stripped off they are drawn to the top of the plan, cut into sections and fed into cookers. At first the cookers were open tanks, little different from the open tryworks used in earlier centuries, and these continued to be used at Grytviken until 1955. The blubber is cut up or 'hogged' and thrown into an open tank where it is cooked with steam for between four and six hours. After cooling, the oil is run out to the separator house where it is centrifuged to remove water and any solid residue.

The advantage of open cooking is that it is carried out at low temperature and pressure which prevents decomposition of the oil and results in a high quality product. Nevertheless, it is a slow and inefficient method and various forms of pressure cookers are now used to speed up the process at the expense of quality. The original pressure cookers were tall cylinders with a door at the top through which lumps of blubber were thrown on to grids below. Steam was fed in at a pressure of 4–5 atmospheres for seven hours to drive the oil out of the blubber. In modern pelagic factories a rotary Kvaener or Hartmann cooker is used. These are horizontal cookers containing a rotating drum with baffles which break up the blubber and facilitate the removal of oil. The process takes only from two to four hours and can be operated continuously, but the oil is of a lower quality.

Meanwhile, on the other side of the plan, the bones are being dragged up a slipway to a large steam saw which cuts them into manageable pieces. These are dropped into a pressure cooker where they are cooked under pressure for twenty hours to express a high quality oil. The solid residue is ground up as bonemeal. The meat, which is also rich in oil, receives a different treatment. After hogging, it is passed down a heated tube by means of a rotary screw where it is cooked sufficiently to make it firm. Liquid is squeezed out in a press and centrifuged, first to remove solids which are put back with the meat and again to remove the oil. The remaining liquid, called glue-water, contains dissolved proteins and is put back with the meat, together with glue-water from the blubber and bones. The resulting sodden mass is passed through a drier and some of the dissolved proteins from the glue-water go back into the meat which is dried and milled into meatmeal.

Only the internal organs now remain on the plan. Depending on the circumstances these may be jettisoned or cooked to yield a poor oil. The whalebone is sometimes collected for making brooms and other articles.

Products from whales pervaded all corners of industry and society, until public opinion and economic pressures began to demand substitutes. Apart from the better-known uses of oil, baleen, meat and bone, the tendons are used in tennis rackets and for surgical stitches, sperm whale teeth are used for piano keys, blood is turned into fertilizer, and the skin of toothed whales makes leather. The liver yields large quantities of Vitamin A (three kilograms of vitamin coming from the liver of a fin whale). The hormones insulin and ACTH, used in the treatment of diabetes and arthritis respectively, are extracted from whale glands. Sperm oil has the greatest multiplicity of uses in dressing leather, in creams, ointments and lotions, as high-grade lubricants and cutting oils, in dyes, detergents, carbon paper and germicides.

A modern whale factory working at full pressure to extract as much from each carcase as efficiently as possible calls for careful management. This is particularly important now that shortage of whales and competition from vegetable oils have cut down the margin of profits. The schedule of the factory has to be organized to fit with the arrival of whales at the slipway so that fuel, which has to be transported a long way to the Antarctic, is not wasted. On the other hand whales cannot be allowed to pile up as the oil in the meat and bones starts to decompose soon after death. If possible, the whale is processed within twenty-four hours of death, and the legal maximum is thirty-three hours. If the meat is going to be used for human consumption, the whale must be cut up earlier, or the catcher crew must slit open the body immediately after death to let the sea cool the body and prevent bacterial decomposition. Antibiotics are also pumped into the carcase to prevent spoilage. Large quantities are needed but they prevent the meat from decaying and preserve the blubber so that a high quality oil is produced.

Since 1965 shore factories have ceased to operate in the Antarctic. They have been wholly superseded by floating factories, which are large ships fitted out to process whales in the manner of shore factories. The first Antarctic floating factory, the *Admiralen,* arrived in southern waters in 1905, only a year after Larsen, and started work at Grytviken. The *Admiralen* and its contemporaries operated in sheltered bays, such as the deep bays of South Georgia, or in the flooded volcanic crater of Deception Island in the South Shetlands. The whales were cut up alongside the ship and the pieces hauled in, a method reminiscent of the old days of whaling and just as hazardous in bad weather.

In 1920 one of these floating factories started work along the ice edge, where the whales congregate, instead of anchoring in a sheltered bay. Its example led the way to the development of pelagic factories, which were floating factories designed for use at sea. They were able to process whales and refuel and service their fleet of catchers far from land.

Two considerations led to the development of pelagic whaling, as this mobile form of operation came to be known. First, it enabled the whalers to hunt among concentrations of whales far from the coastal waters where stocks were already diminishing. To this end, Larsen returned to the Antarctic in command of the pelagic factory *Sir James Clark Ross* to hunt whales in among the ice of the sea that bears Ross's name. The second reason was to avoid control by the British Government.

The shore factories and shore-based floating factories operated in the island groups of the South Shetlands and South Orkneys, along the western coast of Grahamland (now the Antarctic Peninsula), as well as in South Georgia. These all fell into the region of the British Empire known as the Falkland

6

Islands Dependencies and as soon as the factory at Grytviken started work the British Government in the form of the Falkland Islands stepped in to demand rent and royalties. Larsen's company had to pay export duty on each barrel of oil and £250 a year for the lease of the ground on which their factory stood. The British also insisted on certain restrictions designed to control the exploitation of the whale stocks. Each company was allowed to operate only a specified number of catchers and they had to avoid killing females accompanied by calves. As much as possible of each carcase had to be utilized, and at the shore factories this meant the entire carcase.

Outside territorial waters these rules did not apply so 'pirate' whaling companies started to operate with pelagic factories, with established companies following suit as the method proved successful. In 1925, a new kind of factory ship appeared. The *Lancing* had a slipway running through the stern to the main deck which was fitted out as a flensing plan. Whale carcases were brought up to the slipway and seized around the tail flukes by a massive 'Gjeldstad claw' that closed like a pair of tongs and dragged the whale onto the deck. More factory ships of this pattern followed and with the stern slipway and side-by-side funnels leaving room for the whales to be dragged along the centre of the ship, they are as unmistakeable as the oldtime whale-ship with its brick tryworks. They represent the peak of whaling efficiency, cruising in search of whales, guiding their fleet of catchers by radio as reports of schools of whales come in, processing the whales as efficiently as is possible, transferring the products to transport ships, taking on fuel oil from tankers and bunkering the catchers.

Antarctic whaling became a bonanza in the first decades of this century. The Grytviken company was making profits by its second year and new companies hastened southwards, but modern whaling is no more independent of economic and international events than was the Yankee sperm-whaling described in earlier chapters. By 1911 there were eight companies in the field and in 1931 forty-one pelagic factories were operating and 40,201 whales were killed, compared with a hundred and ninety-five in 1904. The result was massive overproduction and a glut of whale-oil. The following year most of the factories were laid up and only seven whaling expeditions went south to the Antarctic. At the same time whaling companies voluntarily agreed to restrict the number of whales killed, not to prevent overkilling and a running down of the stocks, but to prevent overproduction.

After this setback, production crept up again and in 1938 46,039 whales were killed in the Antarctic. World War Two then intervened and only one pelagic factory remained in operation. Most of the others were destroyed, their slow speed making them the lame ducks of the convoy system. After the war there was a great demand for edible animal fats, which the whale industry could supply in the form of hardened whale-oil. The whale stocks had partly recovered during the war years but, despite the braking effect of the International Whaling Commission which was set up in 1946, there has been gross overhunting and Antarctic whaling has gone into decline. The two nations that once dominated the scene, the British and the Norwegians, have given up completely. The Southern Ocean is left to comparative newcomers, the Japanese and Russians. The sad story of the drastic decline of the whale stocks and the unfortunately futile attempts at stemming the steady drain of some species is told in the next chapter.

Throughout this narrative emphasis has been placed on the main branches of the whaling industry: the right-whaling of Spitzbergen, Yankee sperm-whaling, the Arctic bowhead fishery and Antarctic rorqual whaling. While these are the most important stages in the history of whaling it must not be forgotten that lesser enterprises have been continuing all the time, some of which have been described in Chapter 8. In the present century whaling has come to mean the hunting of whales in Antarctic waters as described in this chapter, but at the beginning of the century a few Biscayan right whales were still being killed each year off British coasts and in 1912 Robert Cushman Murphy sailed in the brig *Daisy* on a sperm-whaling voyage, two centuries after Christopher Hussey had killed his first sperm whale.

As whaling flourished in the Antarctic, so did it flourish in other parts of the world. Shore factories once operated in Iceland, Norway, Portugal, Spain, several countries in South America and elsewhere. In the North Pacific, pelagic fleets were for a time catching about half as many whales as the diminished Antarctic expeditions, but as the numbers of the large rorqual species got nearer to the level of extinction, the attention of whalers turned back to sperm whales, which then made up over half the catch of great whales, and to the smaller species such as pilot whales and killer whales. The most recent development has been a swing back to rorquals and the minke whale now make up 80 per cent of the harvest.

The smaller whales and dolphins have always been hunted, and not only by local hunters like the Faeroese and Eskimos. In the latter part of the nineteenth century belugas were hunted extensively off Spitzbergen. Now, however, the refined techniques of modern whaling are bringing increased pressure to bear on the small whales and dolphins and it is becoming worthwhile to catch species that were once not worth the cost of chasing.

When the catches of Antarctic fin whales declined drastically in the 1960s, the whalers turned their attention to the smaller sei whales, which previously had been ignored because of their small size and poor oil yield. The very similar Bryde's whale is also caught. As these species declined, the almost pigmy minke whale became the major target. In the North Atlantic the Norwegians prosecute a vigorous fishery for small whales which yield little oil and are caught for their meat. Some two thousand whales are caught each year in a season that lasts from March to September. They are harpooned from fishing boats and the catch includes minke, killer and pilot whales.

The problem of the small whale fishery is that it is exempt from the regulations that cover the catching of the large whales. As a result the stocks of small whales are being steadily drained. The history of whaling legislation is described in the next chapter and it is almost wholly concerned with the protection of the largest whales. The smaller whales, dolphins and porpoises are not covered by even the limited safeguards given to their larger relatives.

14 | Legislation and Conservation

CONTROL of the whaling industry is not a new idea but until the present century, legislation consisted of those in power attempting to seize as large a share of the catch as possible. Medieval rulers issued laws that claimed stranded whales for their own, acts as selfish as that of demanding treasure-trove. Later, when whaling became an industry, governments tried to assert monopolies over the whaling-grounds. Ownership of the Spitzbergen whaling-grounds was a source of dispute for many years and in 1821 the Russian government tried to exclude foreign whalers from the Bering Sea.

Only when the shares looked as if they were going to disappear was any attempt made to protect the whales. In 1904 the first law preventing the killing of whales was passed. Whaling was banned along the Norwegian coast for the rather bizarre reason that the fishermen believed that fin whales were intimately concerned with the arrival of the herring shoals. A decline in the herring catch led to the 'Menhavn riots' and the Norwegian whalers had to shift their operations to British waters, where they ran into the same trouble.

About this time the Antarctic whaling industry was becoming established and, until the development of pelagic floating factories, all operations were based at stations leased from the Falkland Islands Government. The whaling companies were expected to observe a set of rules that attempted to rationalize the industry and prevent over-exploitation of the whale stocks. Each company was limited in the number of catchers it could employ and the maximum amount of each carcase had to be utilized. The gunners were also to avoid harpooning female whales accompanied by calves.

Pelagic factories rendered these regulations valueless and whaling in the Antarctic proceeded unchecked. In 1925, when the *Lancing* made her first voyage, the total Antarctic catch was 10,488 whales. In 1931 it rose to 40,201 and a consequent glut of whale-oil led the companies to cut down their operations and save themselves from liquidation. The number of floating factories was reduced from forty-seven to seven and the world catch was reduced by over one quarter during the following year. In succeeding years, however, the catch increased again and in 1935 regulations to cut the size of the catch were introduced under the auspices of the League of Nations. In 1937 most whaling nations signed the International Whaling Agreement. These were the first attempts at whaling legislation to be aimed at preservation of whales on an international scale.

The League of Nations regulations formed the basis of subsequent controls on the whaling industry. Like the industry itself, they were concerned primarily with the Antarctic populations of whales. Limits were imposed on the movements of floating factories and the catching of undersize whales was forbidden. The latter rule was designed to eliminate the catching of immature animals, a wasteful act which was very damaging to the whale populations. The size limits were set at 21·34 metres for blue whales and 16·76 metres for fin whales. At the same time the Agreement banned the catching of gray whales and right whales. In 1938 Antarctic humpbacks were also given protection and part of the Southern Ocean was set aside as a sanctuary. Inspectors were appointed to each factory to ensure that the regulations were not flouted.

During World War Two little whaling was undertaken and in 1946 the industry started again almost from scratch. An International Whaling Commission (IWC) was established by the interested nations to work out and administer regulations for the conservation of whale stocks, and thus of the whaling industry as well. The Commission has a scientific committee to collect biological information on the whales and advise on measures to be taken for their preservation. The Commission deliberates on the scientists' recommendations and advises the member governments accordingly.

International bodies for controlling the exploitation of resources are rare, and doubly so when the resource is in international waters, as with whales. The International Whaling Commission is a remarkable body with quite unusual powers, in that measures can be agreed upon by nations with admirable speed. It has great achievements to its credit but it cannot be denied that there are shortcomings in its organization. The members of the IWC do not always agree on every step to be taken and their discussions are not binding on the governments involved. If they object, they can opt out and go their own way.

The composition of the IWC fluctuates as members opt in and out, and not all members hunt whales. Active members, in 1978, were Argentina, Brazil, Chile, Denmark, Iceland, Japan, South Korea, Norway. Peru, Spain and USSR. Unfortunately not all whaling nations belong to the IWC and consequently are not bound by any agreements on quotas or protection. These nations include China and Taiwan, North Korea and Portugal. The total quota by IWC members for 1979/80 was 624 fin whales, 100 sei whales, 743 Bryde's whales, 12,006 minke whales and 2,203 sperm whales. Blue whales, humpbacks, gray whales and right whales are protected except for catches by aboriginal peoples.

Critics of the IWC point out that although it has arranged for the number of whales killed each year to be cut down and has obtained protection for the seriously endangered species, these steps have generally come too late. There are some interested observers who claim that the IWC, far from preserving whale stocks, is presiding over their extinction. These criticisms are largely valid, but the limitations of the IWC's power have to be appreciated. The scientific advisers cannot force their views on the whaling nations, and their arguments are seriously undermined by the lack of knowledge about whale biology and by disagreements among the scientists themselves. As we have seen in the first part of this book, it has not been easy to make the estimates of longevity, birth rate and other factors that are necessary to assess the size of whale populations.

The story of the attempt to limit whaling is depressing; it is a case of shutting a succession of doors after the horse has bolted. In 1944 an agreement was made to limit the numbers of whales killed each year in the Antarctic. A figure was set at two-thirds of the pre-war catch and divided between the participating nations. The size of the catch was calculated in blue whale units (BWU), or the number of blue whales and equivalents in size of oil yield in other species. One blue whale was reckoned to be the equivalent of two fin whales, two and a half humpbacks or six sei whales. In the first year of post-war whaling the quota was set at 16,000 BWU and was made up of a combination of blue whales, fin whales and sei whales.

This method of limiting the catch has an intrinsic drawback in that it gives an overall limit for the numbers of whales caught but no limit for the number from individual species. The result was that each species in turn was attacked until it became rare. The blue whale was the largest and the most profitable species to pursue. Its numbers had already shown a decrease before the war but after the war it was attacked again and it was rare by 1955. As the blue whale became increasingly difficult to find the whalers turned their attention to the fin whale. To achieve the annual quota of BWUs twice as many fin whales had to be killed as the equivalent blue whales, and their numbers dropped rapidly in the early 1960s (Figure 19).

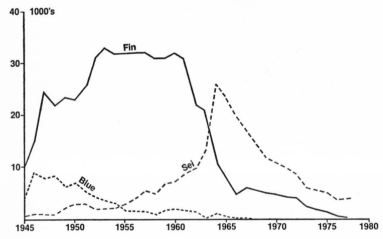

Figure 19 World catch of blue, fin and sei whales. There was a general increase in hunting after World War II. Blue whales soon went into decline and the fin whale catch soared. When the numbers of fin whales dropped, sei whales were caught in increasing numbers.

Then the comparatively small sei whale, which was once shunned as being unprofitable, was hunted and it, too, very soon showed signs of being overhunted.

The postwar overhunting of blue, fin and sei whales has occurred despite the IWC frequently revising the annual Antarctic quota, bringing it down in stages from 16,000 BWUs in 1952 to 2,300 (excluding sperm whales) in 1972.

In 1972 the BWU, which was so obviously useless for proper management, was abandoned in favour of quotas for individual species and, for sperm whales, quotas for each sex. The problem was then to arrive at acceptable quotas. Despite increasing research on the aspects of whale biology which affect breeding – pregnancy rate, growth rate and so on – and the use of sophisticated analytical techniques, there is disagreement among biologists about the levels of exploitation which can be sustained.

The basis of quota-setting is the concept of the Maximum Sustainable Yield (MSY). In a nutshell, a population of animals, such as whales, is generally stable. If the population is reduced by hunting, disease or other catastrophe, it will strive to return to its old numbers through the survivors breeding more rapidly. They start to breed younger and become pregnant more often. (As we have seen on p. 90, a faster breeding does seem to be taking place in exploited whale populations.) When the numbers are restored, breeding is expected to slow down. If, therefore, the population of whales is reduced to the level at which it breeds most rapidly, it can be held at that level by cropping and the 'extra' whales which are being born to raise the population to the old level can be killed without any further decline. In other words, the whalers can take the interest without touching the capital.

This sounds an excellent idea in principle but there are several objections which make the MSY concept unacceptable to many scientists. First, our knowledge of the whales is insufficient to make really accurate assessments of MSYs for various stocks. Then, a population at the MSY level is very vulnerable to other disturbances. It may lose its capacity to recover from a change in climate or alteration in food supplies. It has also been pointed out that the MSY concept considers each species as a separate entity, whereas the various species of whales form parts of the interlocking jigsaw of marine life. A species of whale cannot be considered in isolation and its population is not made up of equal units. Hunting upsets the social system and makes an imbalance in the sex ratio and in the proportion of young to mature animals, which may affect breeding.

The MSY concept may be the best method of whale management we have at the moment, but the replacement of BWUs with species quotas based on MSY has not checked the decline of whales. The species quotas are having to be lowered from year to year, as the BWU limits were before them.

Cuts in the quota often seem to be imposed only when the whalers feel that numbers have already decreased so far that they would be unable to catch many more whales anyway. The failure of the quota system to halt the decline of the whale stocks is shown by the recent inability of the whaling fleets to catch even some reduced quotas. In the 1976-7 season the quota for the southern hemisphere of 20,000 whales of all species was not reached, and the Antarctic fleets (Japanese and Russian) caught only 15,106 whales (206 fin, 1,820 sei, 6,134 minke and 7,046 sperm) between them.

When the whaling industry as a whole has reduced its raw material to a level where it cannot fulfil its own objectives, the inability of the International Whaling Commission to ensure that all the rules governing the protection of whales are observed seems insignificant. There is no doubt that a blind eye is often turned at the factories when a member of a protected species is brought in or if a crooked measurement increases the length of an undersized whale to above the legal minimum.

There was no great cause for alarm when the Antarctic whales first showed signs of diminishing, because it was felt by many whalers that the time would come when there would be too few whales for whaling to pay. As whaling was an expensive business it was thought this would happen before the stocks diminished too far, but the Antarctic whales have virtually disappeared without whaling ceasing. It is now possible to sail through the Southern Ocean without seeing a whale and Ross's account of their abundance quoted in Chapter 13 seems fantastic.

The fact that whaling did not cease some time ago was due to two factors. First, whale products are very valuable, even in the face of competition from fish and vegetable materials.

It is therefore worth mounting expeditions to hunt for the few remaining whales. If necessary, the industry can be bolstered with subsidies. Furthermore, a whaling fleet represents a considerable investment in capital which cannot be easily written off. Whaling operations have, in consequence, been forced to continue and this has been made possible by greater technical efficiency. The catcher boats have increased in size and power; there are improved methods of finding the whales; and a better use is made of the carcases. Despite such efficiency, the boats are chasing fewer whales with diminishing reward.

Table III

	Original stock	Stock remaining today	Percentage remaining today
SOUTHERN HEMISPHERE			
Right	?	3,000	?
Humpback	100,000	3,000	3
Blue	180,000	5,000	3
Fin	400,000	84,000	47
Sei	150,000	53,000	35
Minke	260,000	251,000	96
Sperm male	257,000	128,000	50
female	330,000	259,000	78
NORTH PACIFIC			
Right	?	11,000	?
Humpback	?	1,400	?
Blue	4,900	1,600	32
Fin	43,500	16,000	37
Sei	45,000	21,000	47
Gray	?	11,000	?
Sperm male	195,000	91,000	47
female	152,000	125,000	82

Estimated stocks of whales, as calculated by R. Gambell in 1976. There are no good figures for the North Atlantic but all species are less abundant than in the North Pacific.

It is exasperating to read the reports of the IWC over the last three decades. The scientists of the Commission have managed to amass and analyse a vast body of information on the biology of whales, but the bald statements of the reports show the inability of the whaling nations to agree with the scientists' evidence and reduce the quotas to levels whereby the whale populations will get a chance to recover. On some occasions nations have left the Commission rather than agree to proposals that would damage their short-term interests. It seems that each country wants to play an equally large part in the killing of the goose that lays the golden eggs.

The futility of their actions was shown to the full by figures presented by Dr Mackintosh, one time Director of Research for the Discovery Committee and an expert on whale populations. Dr Mackintosh has shown the extent of the decrease in Antarctic whale stocks. They started to fall in the 1950s and really slumped in the 1960s. He has also shown what would have been the effect of a total ban on whaling at various times in the recent past. If fin whales had been protected in 1960 their numbers would have recovered sufficiently to give a maximum sustainable yield of 20,000 per year by about 1970 (Figure 20). This means that just a few years' idleness by the

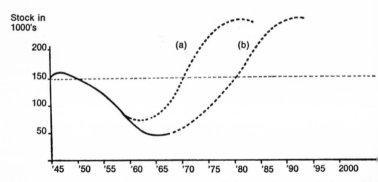

Figure 20 Trends in the population of Antarctic fin whales, after World War II. (a) projected increase if whaling ceased in 1960, (b) projected increase if stopped in 1968. A population of 150,000 would give a sustainable yield of 20,000 (modified from Mackintosh)

whaling fleets, or a few more years on a very restricted quota would have allowed them to revert to pre-war catches. By 1968 the situation had worsened so that a ban would have to be imposed until the early 1980s to have a similar effect. The blue whale has suffered more than the fin whale. It was diminishing sharply before the war, but only in 1965 was it given complete protection. Its survival now seems ensured, although it will take a century or more to recover completely.

The western world, at least, has become conservation-minded but it is still difficult to show many concrete examples of a radical change of attitude towards conservation problems by the people with the power to act, even when these problems concern our daily lives. Despite the protection of whales being a subject of militant international crusades, only in the last year or so have nations engaged in whaling voluntarily closed their whaling industries. It seems ridiculous that the whaling industry should be involved in such a vicious, downward spiral. After all, it is regulated by an international body and the simple fact of over-hunting is plain to see. Nevertheless there remain too many examples of industries still being planned for short term expediency and profit rather than with thought for the future, for us to expect that the whaling industry should behave with rational altruism. Perhaps most of the whale populations are doomed to become scattered remnants before protective measures are taken, in which case we can only hope that they do not linger in the balance like right whales but recover to become tourist attractions like the Californian gray whale.

Since the first edition of this book was published whaling has become the subject of public debate. In 1972, the UN Conference on the Human Environment at Stockholm recommended a ten-year ban on whaling. A meeting of the IWC shortly afterwards rejected the proposal but the event sparked off an intense campaign for whale conservation and protection. In the van there is Greenpeace with its publicity-catching programme of putting human bodies between whale and whaler, while broader-based organizations seek to debate with the whaling interests and develop alternatives to whale products. Perhaps the most notable conservation success has been the banning of whale imports to the United States. On the debit side, there is the emergence of the so-called pirate whalers which operate outside IWC regulations, killing any whale they meet regardless of size, species or whether lactating.

These ships are particularly immoral because their operations can be traced back to countries within IWC.

The whaling question has generated argument and counter-argument and, with emotions often running high, it is not easy to find a disinterested view of affairs. Also, the whole subject of whaling is so complicated that many points of view can be accommodated, which adds to the confusion. The campaign motto of *Save the Whale* was itself a misleading oversimplification. There are many kinds of whales; not all are hunted. Some need protection; others are safe.

When debating the whaling question it is necessary to establish in which arena the argument is to take place. There are four choices: morals, humanity, management and economics.

The morality of taking life, cetacean or otherwise, is very much a matter of individual conscience. For Buddhists the taking of life is abhorrent, whereas Christians have, in the past at least, seen all animals as being placed on earth for Man's benefit and enjoyment. Vegetarians have various reasons for not eating meat. Such sentiments are matters of faith and can only be argued in respect to degree. Is it acceptable to kill animals above a certain level of intelligence? For instance, are the great whales more intelligent than cattle or pigs and is it permissible to kill fish but not warm-blooded mammals?

As to the humane aspect of whaling, there are many people who find the idea of shooting an explosive harpoon into a whale quite reprehensible. Yet, if it kills instantly, a harpoon must provide as good a death as any. However, in the less than ideal conditions of shooting at a moving whale from a bobbing whale-catcher, death often comes slowly. No doubt the whale is in a state of shock but nothing short of instantaneous death is allowed in a slaughterhouse.

If we ignore these two arguments and agree that it is acceptable to hunt and kill whales under present conditions, can the whaling industry justify the present level of exploitation of the whale populations? A Japanese propaganda leaflet asks how westerners would feel if we were told not to kill cattle for food and points out that, as pasture land in their country is limited, the Japanese have to rely on marine food. The obvious retort is that a farmer does not slaughter more cattle than he breeds, and the Friends of the Earth refute the Japanese argument by showing that less than two per cent of the animal protein eaten in Japan came from whales in 1970 (beef provided 7·5 per cent) and animal protein made up only fifteen per cent of total food consumption. The whaling industry would be on firmer ground if it could show that the harvest is not depleting stocks and that management is firmly based on accurate assessments of separate stocks.

There is still dispute about the size of many of the stocks which are currently hunted and whether they are being over-hunted, but, assuming for the moment that whaling is well managed and is taking no more than a sustainable yield, is it economic? The industry contributed only 1·2 per cent of the total harvest from the world's marine resources in 1972. This is a significant drop from the 10·2 per cent share which it had in 1947. Is it worthwhile? This percentage represents a sum of 100 million dollars per year. Globally, this may be a small amount but the whale harvest is still valuable to a company which has its money invested in whaling and a workforce to provide for, while even a single narwhal is of great value to an Eskimo family. Nevertheless, this cannot be a good reason for over-hunting and if the fate of whales has to depend on their commercial value, it should be pointed out that they bring in increasing sums as tourist attractions, either as captives in dolphinaria or as wild animals which can be watched from boats and the shore.

On a scale very different from the activities of the whaling fleets, the hunting of bowheads in Alaskan waters is causing concern to conservationists. The Eskimos of this region have traditionally hunted bowheads and the hunt is part of their culture. They take only a handful of whales each year, but since the bowhead was severely depleted by commercial whalers, this is now a significant fraction. Until 1967, the Eskimos caught about nine whales a year but this number trebled at one time and an unknown number were wounded, or killed and lost. The hunt is exempt from the US Marine Mammal Protection Act but the IWC recommends a total ban because the kill exceeds the rate of replacement by breeding. The United States Government is in an awkward position because it has to defend the Eskimos claim that bowhead whaling is an event essential to their cultural existence (imagine banning a sporting event such as the Derby, at Epsom Downs or Louisville), yet the United States set the world an example by banning whale imports.

The final salvation of the great whales will probably come not from arguments concerning ethics or management, but from a different direction. Increasingly substitutes for whale products are being manufactured from other sources, and provided these substitutes can be produced cheaply and in quantity, the reason for hunting whales should disappear. There are now acceptable substitutes for all whale products and they are gradually being introduced as industries are weaned from their entrenched habits. A notable addition to the range is the liquid wax obtained from two plants: jojoba (pronounced *hohoba*) and crambe or meadow foam, both natives of arid regions in North America. The wax can be substituted for sperm-oil and spermaceti. There is one proviso in the use of substitutes: growing plants to replace whale meat, oil etc will require large acreages of plantations. If this means destroying our already dwindling forests and their wildlife the world environment may be no better off. Similarly, catching Antarctic krill in large quantities instead of the whales which feed on it may put the remaining whales, as well as seals and seabirds, on short commons.

What, then, will be the fate of the great whales? Will the time come when the last lonely whale scours the ocean, calling in vain for its companions, as is already being proclaimed in popular song? My personal feeling is that no species will become extinct, although some local stocks, the equivalent of human races or nations, are already extinct. Those whales which are now being hunted will continue to decline or will not recover until whaling ceases, and 1979 saw the possibility of a moratorium on whales looming albeit distantly. The survivors will then have to contend with increasing pollution and disturbance and whales will never regain the freedom of the seas, any more than lions and elephants will ever range freely again over their former dominions in Africa.

Further Reading

A number of old whaling books are being republished. They make fascinating reading to anyone interested in sailing ships or adventure stories. All books on whale biology necessarily cover much the same ground but this short list gives the most useful works, from which the eager student can progress.

WHALING
The Cruise of the Cachalot, Frank T. Bullen. John Murray, London.
Moby Dick, Herman Melville. J. M. Dent, London.
Old Whaling Days, Captain W. Barron. Conway Maritime Press.
Logbook for Grace, Robert Cushman Murphy. Robert Hale, London.
South Latitude, F. D. Ommaney. Longmans, London.
Whale Manual '78. Friends of the Earth, London.
Penguins, Whalers, and Sealers: A Voyage of Discovery, L. Harrison Matthews. Universe, New York.

WHALES
The Stocks of Whales, N. A. Mackintosh. Fishing News (Books) Ltd.
Whales, E. J. Slijper. Hutchinson, London.
The Natural History of the Whale, L. Harrison Matthews. Weidenfeld & Nicolson, London.

GENERAL
The Whale, ed. L. Harrison Matthews. George Allen & Unwin, London.
Lost Leviathan, F. D. Ommaney. Hutchinson, London.
Marine Mammals, Charles M. Scammon. Dover, New York.

Index